THE RESEARCH-INFORMED TEACHING REVOLUTION

TEACHING REVOLUTION

EARLY YEARS

Edited by

JANE FLOOD &

CHRIS BROWN

JOHN
CATT

First published 2021

by John Catt Educational Ltd,
15 Riduna Park, Station Road,
Melton, Woodbridge IP12 1QT
Tel: +44 (0) 1394 389850
Fax: +44 (0) 1394 386893
Email: enquiries@johncatt.com
Website: www.johncatt.com

ISBN: 978 1 913622 65 7

Set and designed by John Catt Educational Limited

Jane dedicates this book to Lin Stares and Sara Gmitrowicz (awe-inspiring Early Years practitioners to my NQT self), Matt Perrett (for a brilliant Early Years journey to date) and Tina Daniel (for trusting us to go our own research-informed Early Years way).

Chris dedicates this book to Professor Sue Rogers. Thanks for getting me started on my Early Years research journey.

CONTENTS

ACKNOWLEDGEMENTS

Jane and Chris would like to thank the contributors for their fantastic efforts in helping us create what we believe is not only a readable but also a wonderfully powerful book. The pandemic has proved to be both an incredibly disruptive and also an incredibly stressful time for those of us working in education. Despite this, you all stuck with us to deliver your chapters, and we are very grateful that you did!

INTRODUCTION

The importance of play for child development was first theorised by the influential Russian psychologist Vygotsky. He suggested that during play, children exercise control over their mental activity, setting themselves appropriate challenges and creating their own 'zone of proximal development' within which learning is most powerfully enhanced (Vygotsky, 1978, p. 78). More recent research has supported this view. Play has been shown to provide a powerful context for the development of language skills and vocabulary, which in turn support self-regulation (Whitebread, 2015). Leading Early Years theorists, such as Jean Piaget and Maria Montessori, have all ascertained that play is a child's work. Whilst many Early Years practitioners have a good understanding of play theories and child development – the bedrock of Early Years provision – this is often diminished in other areas of the education sector, such as schools or wider society. Here the prevailing language used (for example, 'All they do is just play all day at Nursery' or 'They will start proper learning at big school') devalues the fact that play is how young children learn.

This tension is exacerbated through the organisation of Early Years provision in England. The recently updated non-statutory guidance, *Development Matters*, sets out the standards for learning and development from birth to five years for the Early Years Foundation Stage (EYFS) (Department for Education (DfE), 2020). Alongside this are the statutory Early Learning Goals, which provide a yardstick against which achievement at the end of a child's Reception year can be measured. These developments, which should be in place in all settings by September 2021, are not without criticism. Not giving enough emphasis to play, increasing the emphasis of some of the Early Learning Goals and confusion for practitioners over child development stages are some of the concerns levied at the document (Coalition of Early Years Sector Organisations, 2020). As a result, Birth to 5 Matters is being developed with the Early Years sector, drawing on the existing base of expertise – research evidence and practice knowledge. Its purpose is to support implementation of the statutory EYFS, with an emphasis on providing practitioners with the guidance and further information they want to help them meet children's needs in line with their ethos and pedagogy (The Early Years Coalition).

EYFS often transcends settings, being split across Early Years practitioners (pre-schools, nurseries, childminders, nursery schools and Reception classes), and subsequently difficulties arise through the interpretations of different institutions and a lack of shared language. Most young children begin the EYFS in a nursery or pre-school setting and then transfer to schools for the final year (known as Reception) in the September after their fourth birthday. Whilst the professionals in these settings often work together to ensure a smooth transition – and for some children, the Foundation Stage is a continuation, as they attend a nursery attached to a school – this 'break' in the Foundation Stage is challenging. Schools can be very rigid organisations, operating set times at which children are required to attend, whereas day nurseries and pre-schools offer a more flexible pattern of attendance to reflect the needs and wishes of the parents and families. Although there is a shared non-statutory framework, there is little time or opportunity for nurseries, pre-schools and Reception teachers to work together on professional development, curriculum design, moderation and assessment outside of pockets of locally organised initiatives.

The situation is compounded by the current accountability system in England. Statutory baseline assessments undertaken in the first few weeks after a child starts school (or at the beginning of their final year in EYFS) are required and submitted to the DfE. This in turn provides data which is subsequently used to measure progress of children throughout primary school. These 'tests' are at odds with the many theories associated with child development and play (as well as the values and beliefs of Early Years practitioners) because of the focus on the more easily measured knowledge-based elements of the EYFS (for example, language, communication and literacy and mathematics). It is far harder to measure the three prime areas identified in the Foundation Stage – 1) Personal, Social and Emotional Development (PSED); 2) Communication and Language; and 3) Health and Self-Care – using such metrics. It is even more challenging to consider the Characteristics of Effective Learning, the underpinning pedagogy of the Foundation Stage curriculum. In addition, this can be considered another example of the fractured Foundation Stage, where all the observations and assessments of children undertaken by the previous setting over several years are all but ignored. This situation can result in practitioners feeling under pressure for children to achieve; yet as research tells us, learning is not linear (Stewart, 2015). Nor does formal learning usually start so young (Dubiel and Kilner, 2017). This leads us back to the theme of the opening section of this chapter that play is indeed a child's work.

As a result, practitioners need to be skilled to recognise, understand and deal with these tensions in the system; and becoming research-informed is a possible approach that can help here. A salutary reminder of this was the publication of *Bold beginnings* (2018) by Ofsted, which provided an empirical analysis of 41 good and outstanding schools, selected because they performed highly against a range of indicators, including EYFS development levels, the phonics screening check and attainment at Key Stage 1 (Mujis, 2018). A swift rejoinder from the Association for Professional Development in Early Years (TACTYC) suggested that the report had cherry-picked evidence and that Early Years is a distinct curriculum – not just a preparation for Key Stage 1 (and the National Curriculum). To counteract such claims presented in reports such as *Bold beginnings*, TACTYC suggested that '[a]ll reception teachers need robust, research-informed understanding of child development, curriculum and pedagogy appropriate to young children' (TACTYC, p. 2). The reference to Reception teachers is in response to the focus of *Bold beginnings*, but could extend to include all Early Years practitioners.

That Early Years professionals might benefit from becoming research engaged follows other similar developments in the field of education. In recent years there has been a growing commitment towards all educational practitioners using rigorous research evidence to improve the quality of teaching and subsequently student outcomes (Brown, Flood and Handscomb, 2020). In addition to school improvement, the use of research can aid professional development (ibid.), lead to improved decision-making and provide greater job satisfaction for practitioners. Yet becoming research-informed is a challenge, and practitioners face many barriers such as time, opportunities and access to relevant quality research (Brown, 2015). For example, some of the available research is of mixed quality and relevance. Some areas – such as the importance of play for young children's development – have a strong bank of evidence to draw upon, while it proves harder to locate quality evidence that is relevant in others, such as imaginative role play. Practitioners also need the necessary research literacy skills to unpick research that is offered, assessing its relevance to their context and the robustness of the research design. The aforementioned *Bold beginnings* provides a case in point here: the study was a relatively small-scale study and showcased non-representative findings from 41 Reception class settings in schools deemed good or outstanding by Ofsted. In other words, these schools were selected because of their high performance against a range of indicators (such as EYFS development levels, Year 1 phonics screening checks and attainment at Key Stage 1), and therefore the findings might not be applicable to all settings.

This book represents a collection of think pieces from a variety of people with a wealth of Early Years knowledge and experience, all committed to driving improvement in Early Years education through being research-informed. It is intended to support anyone who is involved in Early Years in understanding what it means to become research-informed and what this might look like in practice. The second in a series of research-informed books edited by us, the focus on Early Years was conceived at a local BrewED Early Years event which took place days before the first national lockdown in March 2020 during the COVID-19 pandemic. This event, organised by David Wright (a contributor to this collection), united practitioners from nurseries, pre-schools and Reception classes, school leaders, consultants and academics in professional learning and research-informed discussion for a day of talking and reflecting on all things Early Years. Little did we know at that time that it was to be the last professional face-to-face learning many of us would be able to participate in for many months, or that many settings were to face extreme challenges in the coming weeks.

We have organised the book as follows. The first section reflects on the benefits of Early Years practitioners becoming research-informed. Here authors such as Aaron Bradbury and Sue Allingham provide strong arguments for researched-informed practice in Early Years. Aaron, for instance, suggests that research should help practitioners become critical of and reflective on what they are doing and why, whilst similarly Sue recommends practitioners should challenge their thinking through becoming research-informed and engaging with evidence that may run contrary to their philosophy. The chapters by Kristina Westlund and Katie Sears both provide an international perspective for practitioners on what using research in practice might look like in an Early Years setting. Kristina offers insights from an action research project in Sweden, whilst Katie discusses her own use of research to aid her own professional development and how this has looked in her current role as a Reception teacher in Hong Kong. David Wright continues the theme of professional development as he charts his own research journey – imploring the reader to always be curious – and what this has meant for the nurseries he runs. Alistair Bryce-Clegg reflects on his own experiences of becoming research-informed through further study that has equipped him to question dominant discourses in education and the motivations needed to become an active user of research evidence. This section concludes with Alexandra Harper offering an Australian perspective on the benefit of teacher accreditation as a way of becoming research-informed.

The next section focuses on specific themes within Early Years education and the importance of engaging with high-quality and relevant research to develop thinking, innovate and reflect on these changes. Dominic Wyse's chapter on children's agency and the curriculum provides the starting point of this section and uses the Early Years curriculum as a suitable starting point to raise complex questions about the place of research in relation to practice and policy. With classroom practice firmly in mind, both in terms of indoor and outdoor provision, the next two chapters consider how research was used to develop two innovative projects. Firstly, Shonette Bason-Wood provides an insight into a movement-based approach to early writing and how research helped her develop this in an age-appropriate (and fun) way. Another popular Early Years theme – learning outdoors – is explored by Julie Mountain, as she describes the research-inspired project Learning through Landscapes. Julie highlights the benefits of working with other stakeholders, in this instance academics, to aid knowledge acquisition and to act as a critical friend. In their chapter Jane Flood and Matt Perrett continue this theme, describing the impact of being involved in a Research Learning Community facilitated by a Teaching School Alliance in partnership with an academic and the subsequent changes to outcomes for summer-born children that have occurred. The notion of working in partnership with other stakeholders – in the context of Early Years the importance of working with parents – is subsequently explored in the next two chapters. Janet Goodall explains clearly the importance of using research for professional development and making changes to practice in the context of parental engagement. Then Gina Sherwood picks up many of these themes in her chapter, which provides an example of how to carry out research on partnership relationships with parents and carers in your setting. Leadership can provide the supportive conditions needed for the Early Years sector to become research-informed, suggests Lewis Fogarty in the penultimate chapter. Lewis offers the Four Pillars of Pedagogy framework that leaders in settings and schools can use to reflect, support, develop and celebrate their own practice.

We finish with a chapter written by Professor Sue Rogers that both expands upon and corrals the ideas presented, and which provides some final food for thought on how you can link research and teaching within and across Early Years settings. We, the editors – having read all the chapters that comprise this book – feel that they are packed with insight and that, in bringing the book together, we have produced something truly comprehensive. But, as ever, we try not to assume, so if you think a key idea or case study is still out there (or even if you think another aspect of teaching would benefit from the 'Revolution' focus), we'd love to hear from you!

REFERENCES

Association for Professional Development in Early Years (TACTYC) (2017). Bold beginnings: A Response to Ofsted's (2017) report, Bold beginnings: The Reception curriculum in a sample of good and outstanding primary schools. Retrieved from https://tactyc.org.uk/wp-content/uploads/2017/12/Bold-Beginnings-TACTYC-response-FINAL-09.12.17.pdf.

Brown, C. (ed.) (2015). *Leading the use of research and evidence in schools*. London: IOE Press.

Brown, C., Flood, J. and Handscomb, G. (2020). *The research-informed teaching revolution: A handbook for the 21st century teacher*. Woodbridge: John Catt Educational.

Centre for Research in Early Childhood (2020). Birth to 5 Matters – feedback from CREC's consultation event. Retrieved from http://www.crec.co.uk/announcements/B25M-consultation-event-feedback.

Coalition of Early Years Sector Organisations' statement on the new non-statutory guidance for the EYFS (2020). Retrieved from https://www.early-education.org.uk/press-release/coalition-early-years-sector-organisations-statement-new-non-statutory-guidance-eyfs.

Department for Education (2020). Development Matters: Non-statutory curriculum guidance for the early years foundation stage. Retrieved from https://assets.publishing.service.gov.uk/government/uploads/system/uploads/attachment_data/file/944603/Development_Matters_-_non-statuatory_cirriculum_guidance_for_EYFS.pdf.

Dubiel, J. and Kilner, D. (2017). Teaching four and five year olds: The Hundred Review of the Reception year in England. Early Excellence publication. Retrieved from https://tactyc.org.uk/wp-content/uploads/2017/06/EX_TheHundredReview_Report_.pdf.

Grenier, J. (2019). What happened to curriculum in the early years? Retrieved from https://impact.chartered.college/article/what-happened-to-curriculum-early-years/?utm_campaign=1639547_12.%20December%20 2%202020%20early%20career%20members.&utm_medium=email&utm_ source=Chartered%20College%20of%20Teaching&dm_t=0,0,0,0,0.

Ofsted (2018). Bold beginnings: The Reception curriculum in a sample of good and outstanding primary schools. Retrieved from https://assets.publishing. service.gov.uk/government/uploads/system/uploads/attachment_data/ file/663560/28933_Ofsted_-_Early_Years_Curriculum_Report_-_ Accessible.pdf.

Mujis, D. (2018). Bold beginnings and the importance of reception. Retrieved from https://researched.org.uk/2018/07/04/bold-beginnings-and-the-importance-of-reception-3/.

Stewart, N. (2015). Development Matters: A landscape of possibilities not a road map. Retrieved from https://eyfs.info/articles.html/teaching-and-learning/ development-matters-a-landscape-of-possibilities-not-a-roadmap-r205/.

The Early Years Coalition (2021). Birth to 5 Matters: Non-statutory guidance for the Early Years Foundation Stage. Retrieved from https://www.birthto5matters. org.uk/wp-content/uploads/2021/03/Birthto5Matters-download.pdf.

Vygotsky, L. S. (1978). *Mind in society: The development of higher psychological processes*. Cambridge, MA: Harvard University Press.

Whitebread, D. (2015). Play and Self-regulation. Play in Education Development and Learning. Retrieved from https://www.pedalhub.org.uk/play-piece/play-and-self-regulation.

FROM BEING TO BECOMING – EARLY YEARS EDUCATION AND RESEARCH WITHIN PRACTICE

AARON BRADBURY

Aaron Bradbury is an Early Childhood Academic, paying close attention to all aspects of Early Years and child-centred practice, workforce development, child development and research.

His current role is that of Principal Lecturer for Childhood and Early Years at Nottingham Trent University, based within the Institute of Social Sciences.

RESEARCH IN PRACTICE

You always hear how research needs to be practice-informed within the Early Years. But how much research is truly practice-informed? I would be wrong if I said that all the research I do is taken 100 per cent from professionals working with children. But how do we move research into practice? Firstly, we (academics and leaders within education) must advocate for practitioners to expand within their experience by engaging in research. Early Years educators are continually doing this within their practice through daily enquiry, evaluation and investigation. So we must not make research a 'scary' thought – something that is done on a whim or not done at all. Practice-based research is the aim of what I am going to be discussing here, and I will then refocus the discussion around becoming research-informed.

There are many aspects of my role as a researcher that allow me to discuss certain areas of research and how to relate these to Early Years teaching practice. There are many factors which have allowed me to successfully move research into my own practice, and this has been reinforced through a reflective approach. Becoming a reflective practitioner allowed me to think critically about certain points within my own practice, thus providing me with the time and space to think about the 'why' and 'what if' scenarios within the classroom environment. I call this 'positioning us for research'. Work-based research has to take into account the many ways in which the work of professionals within the Early Years landscape has changed and is continually changing. You could argue that there is some certainty within Early Years education and that we may always need to adapt, respond to change and continually improve because of policy reviews and directives throughout the UK. These place a high level of expectation on the teacher/professional through target setting and professional expectations. Trying to be research-informed on top of this might seem to be an expectation too far. So let's break this down and let me tell you how I overcame these hurdles.

Undertaking research was not something that happened naturally for me, just like it may not happen naturally for you either. Most research comes from the interconnectivity involved in being interested in something. For me, it was the desire to know about what the child was thinking and the reason behind why children did things in certain ways. At the same time, I was also interested in how we as adults supported children's learning and development and held on to the principles underlying outcomes for the child. Ultimately, my early research was carried out through observations and evaluations within the classroom setting – it had to happen somewhere. But it was how I was interpreting what I had seen that mattered most. You get the feeling that you want to know more, so you head for the books and then this gives you further scope to go and read journals. It was this element of reading about child development and then seeing it in reality that got me thinking critically. Reading is an important aspect of research; you start to read critical writing that transforms your own critical thinking processes. I started asking questions and then began to associate the current literature with what I was seeing in practice. This was when the light-bulb moment happened!

BEING RESEARCH-INFORMED IN THE EARLY YEARS

Being research-informed within your practice allows you to link the theoretical approaches and research with practice, which ultimately informs pedagogy in your Early Years setting. There are many ways we know this happens. Take for example the Effective Provision of Pre-School Education (EPPE) project (Sylva et al., 2004), which provides clear evidence alongside endorsement concerning the impact on the pre-school provision. You could also reason that the Early Years Foundation Stage (2017) (EYFS) was founded on research around the child, child-initiated play and adult strategies with regard to supporting the child.

Being research-informed allows you to identify and recognise excellence within your teaching, but also to recognise the value that is placed upon the child. Becoming research-informed means that you are exploring how research and evidence are used to further support optimal decision-making within your practice. The knowledge that you have found can then be used within your own practice to support other colleagues too.

Early Years educators increasingly seek to base their classroom practice on a wide range of current research in education, neuroscience and cognitive psychology. All of this allows us as educators to understand how children acquire and retain knowledge so that they have an understanding of their world. Being research-informed allows you to be a continual learner within your role, by allowing both reflection and continuing professional self-development. These are my essentials when becoming research-informed:

1. Learning should be relational. It is not just about the learning between you and the child, but also the learning that is taking place within the environment, allowing for collaboration and the promotion of discussion and debate – ultimately the skills that are required for research.

2. Motivation. Being motivated and ready to take on the next steps of reading to inform your practice is essential to moving towards becoming research-informed.
3. Learning with reflection. Learning takes place when there is a place for reflection. So taking time out to reflect on your practice is important – a time to review and become critical within your teaching practice.
4. Learning becomes enhanced. Enhancement of concepts and theories supports your learning, self-awareness, ideas and further research concepts.
5. Deep learning. Research or positioning yourself for learning will allow you to look deeper into your own learning and become ready to be research-informed or to take the lead in doing some of your own research.

To put it simply, being research-informed is about critically engaging with research that shapes and helps children and knowing which research does not do this. Being able to use this knowledge within your practice and in your organisational decision-making is important so that you can use evidence-based research that allows positive outcomes for all children. It can be supported by one person or can be the collective ethos of your setting or even the wider context of a group of settings. The main thing is that you need to start small and make connections where research is happening in depth, for example, through research schools; communities of practice; your local universities; and by getting hold of research journals. One way this has changed more recently is through the introduction of membership organisations, which have allowed members to have access to a wide range of journals. However, research can be obtained for free by using different apps and websites, such as ResearchGate. This is an online platform where published material is shared by the authors, making accessibility to evidence-based research even easier.

There are multiple situations arising from your daily role where there are opportunities to respond in a manner that is informed by further research. Research is normally derived from an area of your practice that has some meat on its bones. What I am trying to explain here is that your research needs to have some meaning. There is no need to use or undertake research if you know the answer in advance, or where research has been published and already provides you with the answers. Research should be new knowledge for you and the sector as a whole – something that is bringing new concepts, ideas and dialogue.

Let's look at the diagram below and allow ourselves to put research and practice together by linking both research and Early Years practice. What the diagram is highlighting is that both need to complement each other.

Authentic Meaningful Research

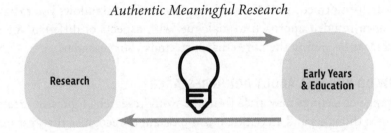

For me, being research-informed within your practice goes hand in hand with being an academic. I guess we are all academics in our own way. I feel that our profession has two different but complementary aspects to it, where Early Years education works in combination with research. Let's be honest, who would want to be part of a profession where new knowledge is not being created?

POSITIONING YOURSELF FOR RESEARCH

There has been a large push for research since I was in the classroom, and there has been a significant increase in research-informed settings. It is an interesting concept that there is a growing need for Early Years educators to start being research-informed. But you need to reflect on your positionality and the approach that you are taking. Firstly, you need to know that you are not going to be right all of the time. We see this continually with educators who have read certain articles and then adopt certain aspects of what is stated, thinking this is the only way to do something. The stark reality is that it may not be. My approach to overcoming this would be to read even further, look at articles that oppose certain aspects, make an informed decision and allow myself to be open to criticism – harsh, but a reality when you want to engage in research. The biggest learning curve for me is that there will always be someone who disagrees with what you have written. And you know what? That is OK. Move on and use their viewpoints to inform your next output or try it out and see for yourself. Getting a balance before you approach any area of research is important. You may not always agree with certain articles, but this is one important aspect of becoming research-informed. You also need to be aware that this allows you to have an open-minded approach to dialogue, with aspects of different voices and ideas becoming the norm that surrounds your research.

HOW DO YOU FEEL ABOUT DOING RESEARCH?

A range of feelings may arise from the word 'research'. I guess it creates its own thoughts and anxieties. It is important to recognise that research is a tool (MacNaughton et al., 2010), and, as with any tool, you start to learn about what it does and that you are the one using it, so you become in control of using it.

There are many misconceptions/myths/stereotypes associated with the word 'research'. So let's take a look at some of the misconceptions that can prevent Early Years professionals from participating in their own research process:

- The research process is intellectual, complex and time-consuming, so people like me cannot possibly do it.
- There is only one way to do research.
- Research is boring.
- Research is only linked to science.
- Research only produces hard facts which you can't question.
- Early Years research can only be done by academics.

IN REALITY – EARLY YEARS RESEARCH IN PRACTICE

Below is a list of some inclusive ways to view research within your practice:

- You already possess many everyday research skills.
- Research can be undertaken by anyone – including Early Years colleagues.
- Research can be a tool for you to use.
- Research can be fun and a recognition of your hard work.
- The researcher asks questions that really matter.
- Research develops your knowledge.
- Research allows you to change your practice and it improves your practice.
- Research allows us to understand the complexities within the Early Years.
- Research can benefit you, your work, the child and your work setting.

You must find your own stance when it comes to research. It is important to mention here that research is not for everyone, and even though you may want to work towards a more research-informed approach, some people may take a little longer to recognise their position within the research process or why they need to engage. You may be wondering what you can add to Early Years research and whether your voice is going to be taken seriously. The great news is that Early Years research is a rapidly expanding area that you can contribute to, and you *can* become a practice-informed researcher.

PRINCIPLES OF EARLY YEARS RESEARCH

I feel that it is important to mention here that research did not come naturally to me at first, and I have had to work at it over the past 10 years. Neither did the expertise in writing effectively with regard to debate, becoming critical and writing with rigour regarding subjects within my field. Regardless of your research projects, there are some basic principles that I have followed to underpin all of the quality elements of

my Early Years research. These were outlined to me when completing my research as part of my Master's degree, and can be summarised as follows (MacNaughton et al., 2010).
Your research should:

- be critical
- be ethical
- respect the child's participatory rights
- be well designed
- have a purpose
- demonstrate honesty about your assumptions.

Let me explain why being honest about your assumptions is important. Assumptions in your research are things that are somewhat out of your control, but your study would become irrelevant if they disappeared. For example, if you are doing a study on Early Years music, there is an underlying assumption that music will be an important continuation aspect within the Early Years. If you are asking people to fill in surveys or answer questions as part of an interview, you will assume that they will answer truthfully. Leedy and Ormrod (2010) posited that '[a]ssumptions are so basic that, without them, the research problem itself could not exist' (p. 62). You cannot just simply state that these are the assumptions you are making. Instead, you need to be able to justify how each assumption is 'probably' true. To assume, for example, that participants will answer honestly, you can explain how anonymity and confidentiality will be preserved and that the participants are volunteers who may withdraw from the study at any time and with no ramifications.

MY GREATEST SUCCESS

I have come a long way from my days of teaching in the Early Years. In fact, it wasn't when I was working with children that my research started; it was when I was working in the Local Authority. This role required me to look at data – numbers on a spreadsheet and lists and names of certain groups of children. This made me start questioning the fact that these children, in a service I was leading at the time, were in fact not being seen or heard and were literally a number on a spreadsheet. I won't lie; this time was hard; we were making decisions based on numbers rather than hearing from the children themselves about their experience. I decided to start using the skills that I had learnt from my Master's degree and I set up a community of practice. This was a process that involved listening to the families and children and allowing them to meet with me and the team to explore the true meaning of gaining the voice of children. It was a simple explanation of listening to the families and children and allowing them to meet with me and the team to explore what gaining the voice of children truly meant.

The important element of this research was what I did with the information I had collected. I was able to quickly turn the information into four key themes. I was able to write a report and gain an insight into the children's lives in the Local Authority. What I didn't realise at the time was that this process had in fact been a mini research project. Gaining the data; being sensitive and making sure that all the information was confidential; carefully considering how we gained the information; and what it was we were doing with the information were all key factors in my approach. I feel that this is where my thirst to know more was born, and I am now writing and teaching research and am on my way to gaining a Doctorate in Education. One point that I want you to take away from this is to 'have a go', and as long as you do not cause ethical conflict with your subjects, then keep having a go and question absolutely everything.

CONCLUSION

This chapter is a description of how to position yourself for starting your research journey. Research isn't as scary as you might think, and the chapter has highlighted many reasons why it is important to engage in research to inform your practice. But most importantly, you are the next generation of researchers and should be using the voice of children to support those children in making the most of their education. I truly believe that you are engaging in research every day, but you need to start thinking about what you would do if you were going to write about it. Gaining a principled position as an Early Years educator is an important aspect of both teaching and research. Becoming critical thinkers with the ability to challenge evidence robustly, and adopting an ethical stance when you are starting your research journey, are important aspects to me, and I would recommend adhering to these principles when undertaking research.

TOP TIPS

Here are my three tips to being able to move forward with research:

- Be brave and explore everyday teaching practices for child-centred outcomes; don't lose sight of why you are doing it.
- Become critical of and reflective about what you are doing. Are you doing this because you have always done it this way?
- Engage with research projects at higher education institutions and explore your own continuing professional development journey in research.

REFERENCES

Department for Education (2017). Statutory Framework for the Early Years Foundation Stage. Retrieved from https://www.gov.uk/government/publications/early-years-foundation-stage-framework--2.

Leedy, P. D. and Ormrod, J. E. (2010). *Practical research: Planning and design*, 9th edition. New York, NY: Merrill.

MacNaughton, G., Rolfe, S. and Siraj-Blatchford, I. (eds) (2010). *Doing early childhood research: International perspectives on theory and practice*, 2nd edition. Buckingham: Open University Press.

Sylva, K., Melhuish, E., Sammons, P., Siraj-Blatchford, I. and Taggart, B. (2004). The Effective Provision of Pre-School Education (EPPE) Project: Final Report: A Longitudinal Study Funded by the DfES 1997–2004.

'DO YOU THINK YOUR METHODS WORK?'

DR SUE ALLINGHAM

Sue Allingham comes to this chapter from a background of teaching across the primary stage, but specialising in Early Childhood Education (ECE). Through her teaching she became a Senior Lead for Early Years in a primary school and a Lead Teacher for her Local Authority. This led her to completing an MA in ECE with the University of Sheffield. She describes this as a pivotal moment.

Sue says her role in the Local Authority gave her the confidence to apply for an Early Years Advisory role in a neighbouring Local Authority: 'I went on to do a doctorate in ECE and the rest, as they say, is history.'

INTRODUCTION

The idea of 'research-informed teaching' had not occurred to me until I embarked on my Master's. Up until then I had taught all the children I'd met using a mixture of my teacher training and my own thinking along the way. I read the usual magazines, but not really any books. I joined Early Education, which was then the British Association of Early Childhood Education, which really fed my thinking and professional development. This, of course, was research, but I hadn't seen it like that. As I said, the MA was the pivotal moment where everything suddenly made sense in my practice. During this time, my then Deputy Head took me to one side and said, 'Sue, do you think your methods work?'

Having tracked successive Reception classes through to Year Six, I knew that they did, and it had never occurred to me that they didn't. Well, not consciously anyway. I spent a great deal of time reflecting on my practice and provision so that I could provide an 'enabling environment'. It was this question that stayed in the back of my mind through my doctoral research and my career as an Early Years Adviser for a Local Authority. It now drives me in my role as an independent consultant and author, and it will drive this chapter through three lenses:

- What?
- Why?
- How?

Definition of terms

Throughout this piece I will refer to 'teachers'. By this term I mean everyone who works within the field of Early Childhood Education, whatever their age or background and whether or not they have qualifications. This is because we are all teachers the minute that children enter our settings. The children are immediately learning something from us.

> The environment you construct around you and the children also reflects this image you have about the child. There's a difference between the environment that you are able to build based on a preconceived image of the child and the environment that you can build that is based on the child you see in front of you — the relationship you build with the child, the games you play. (Malaguzzi, 1993)

I'll come back to this thinking of a 'preconceived idea'.

WHAT DOES IT MEAN TO BE 'RESEARCH-INFORMED'?

The expression 'research says…' is used regularly across our profession. In my experience it is used in one of two ways. It can be used in a closed way, such as, 'Research says it must be done like this, so we have to do it', or it can be used in an open way, such as, 'I've read something that I think might be useful. I wonder what research there is about it?'

Unfortunately, it is often the former that dictates practice and provision. As noted in the introduction, my personal experience was of my reflective ways being questioned.

So, what is this holy grail of 'research'? The *Oxford English Dictionary* definition states that research is:

n. The systematic investigation into and study of materials and sources in order to establish facts and reach new conclusions.

v. carry out research into.

use research to discover or verify information presented in (a book, programme, etc.).

This is exciting and enticing, full of opportunities and avenues to investigate. Who wouldn't want to 'establish facts and reach new conclusions'? Research isn't a static thing that finally decides the way something is done; it is something that is done in order to gain greater depth of understanding to inform what we do. Without this type of thinking, nothing would ever move forward.

The ways in which this research is done are many and various. Every time you enter your place of work, whatever type of provision you have, you are a researcher. You are noticing things and acting on them. Something might happen that completely alters your perspective that day. Every day we encourage the children to investigate and explore their thinking. We are actively encouraged through our statutory obligation to inform our work through the Characteristics of Effective Teaching and Learning:

1.15 In planning and guiding what children learn, practitioners must reflect on the different rates at which children are developing and adjust their practice appropriately. Three characteristics of effective teaching and learning are:

- playing and exploring – children investigate and experience things, and 'have a go'
- active learning – children concentrate and keep on trying if they encounter difficulties, and enjoy achievements
- creating and thinking critically – children have and develop their own ideas, make links between ideas, and develop strategies for doing things. (DfE, 2020, p. 17)

When Dame Clare Tickell proposed these 'characteristics' in her report in 2011, it was clear that there was an expectation that the workforce would be well informed:

> 3.29 *All early years practitioners will need to understand the different ways in which children learn, in order to provide effective support.* While implicit in the current EYFS, I believe the EYFS would be a better product if these were made explicit. I therefore recommend that playing and exploring, active learning, and creating and thinking critically, are highlighted in the EYFS as three characteristics of effective teaching and learning, describing how children learn across a wide range of activities. These characteristics are drawn from the commitments of the EYFS and describe how children learn rather than what they learn. They begin at birth and are lifelong characteristics which need to be fostered and developed during the early years as they are critical for building children's capacity for future learning. (Tickell, 2011, pp. 27–28) (*my italics*)

We cannot be well informed unless we engage in research of our subject area. Unless we understand how children learn, how can we effectively understand the following statement?

> These characteristics are drawn from the commitments of the EYFS and describe how children learn rather than what they learn. (Tickell, 2011, pp. 27–28)

But how do we know how and what to read, act on, go to training about, or listen to? And do we need to anyway? Notice that Dame Tickell takes it as read that all teams working within Early Childhood Education have a good knowledge of child development. In this way they will be able to filter their practice through their knowledge. Whilst this can be the case, it often isn't. I am in no way apportioning blame to those working with the youngest children, as this problem can happen when teachers are moved around in schools and they change from other key stages. However, a move into the Early Years is not as easy as perhaps it sounds for those with no background in Early Childhood Education. In this way research becomes an integral part of the role.

The problem with any sort of research into any phase of education, but maybe particularly teaching and learning in Early Childhood Education, is that it tends to be qualitative and less easy to quantify. The how, what and why are less easily demonstrated to those without a background in the subject. For example, when I was a Local Authority Early Years Adviser, I was questioned by a Primary Adviser about the work I was doing with a school we were both supporting. The Early Years Team had worked so hard on their practice and provision and the children were getting so much more from it. All my observations showed this. However, the Primary Adviser wanted quantifiable evidence in percentages and hard data. Of course, this wouldn't be available until the end of the Reception Year. Without spreadsheets of data, my work and that of the Early Years Team was somehow seen as not significant.

This despite the amount of 'action research' that had gone into the work being done, which involved the collection, organisation and analysis of information, establishing facts to increase understanding of a topic or issue and to reach new conclusions, as described in the definition of 'research' I provided earlier.

DIFFERENT TYPES OF RESEARCH

I have already mentioned the expression 'research says' and how it is used and abused. This problem is compounded by the fact that what qualifies as 'research' can be very broad. By saying that research is integral to working in education, we do not mean that all teachers must spend all their free time buried in books and extra training.

I've reflected on the 'action research' that the School Early Years Team and I did together to improve practice and provision. We were all involved, and it was not a specific programme or plan that we just 'did to' the children. In this way it was integral and not a 'bolt on'. There are many such 'bolt on' programmes available, sometimes handed down centrally as something that we are recommended to do. Any internet search or scrutiny of social media threads will give examples of these packages. In this way ideas are perpetuated and become relied upon. I have recently seen a request for research on a particular topic met with responses recommending some Facebook groups and blogs. Is this 'research'? Well, to an extent it is, because it is reading to further knowledge. However, in some cases blogs and Facebook groups are just perpetuating an opinion that really has little depth or background. But even following these up is research, because it will cause us to reflect on what we do despite realising that the ideas are really 'fads' or 'trendy'. Such references are often obvious because the blogs or groups are trying to sell us something – an 'approach' that will work for your children. Your 'how, what, why' lenses are crucial at this point. Some readers may remember the overnight sensation of 'Brain Gym' some years ago. We all had to train in it and do the sequence of exercises with our classes every day in order to enhance their brain power. This has long since been debunked as a fad:

> Brain Gym and Edu-K [come] out of the same tradition of the [1970s] – using physical movements to improve the brain. In the previous 3–4 decades there has been no empirical evidence to support the claims of Edu-K. This is a pattern we see in pseudosciences over and over again. Years and decades go by without the promoters of these dubious methods providing the evidence that would convince an appropriately skeptical scientific community. They have no legitimate excuses for this lack of evidence – even after years, and even after making substantial sums of money on their methods. (Novella, 2008)

Unfortunately, the world of education is awash with pseudoscience. And it is all too easy to fall into the trap of 'bolting it on' to our practice. So, with all this in mind, why couldn't the Primary Adviser understand the strength and value of qualitative research? The basis of this is in Malaguzzi's notion of a 'preconceived idea' of the child.

This 'preconceived idea' becomes a 'one size fits all' way of thinking that is underpinned by what Archer (2020) calls 'what works research'. He defines this as follows:

Much of the research which falls under this approach is based on seeking to improve a finite set of pre-determined outcomes (primarily in literacy, numeracy and science) and is informed by questions of 'how' these outcomes can be achieved rather than 'why'. This 'howness' is seen in the idea of, and the push to understand, causes by means of experimental research in order to secure findings.

Notice the quantifiable nature of 'outcomes'. Just as the Senior Adviser wanted. She was looking for assessment data of some sort to prove and validate the quality of the work done. However, what we had was observations and soft data which proved a point categorically. Does this make qualitative research less important or valid? As Archer (2020) points out:

If ideas of 'what works' come to dominate perspectives of research in early childhood education, we risk losing numerous other world views in multiple contexts which inform our research work and consequently our practice as researchers and practitioners.

ONE SIZE FITS ALL

Archer points out that 'we risk losing numerous other world views' if we only work towards researching a set of predetermined outcomes. If we have already decided what the outcomes 'must' be (as in the expression 'age related expectations', for example), we have already limited the research and any learning from it. If we are looking to become research-informed teachers, we have to move away from such an approach. This is not easy, as we are bombarded with it through policy and guidance. An informed, pedagogical approach to Early Childhood Education is not about the children scoring on a 'baseline test' or a 'good level of development (GLD)' on the Early Years Foundation Stage Profile; it's about researching into why things happen.

Jack was in one of my Reception classes. He loved investigating how things worked and were done. We were building a life-sized robot from cardboard and chicken wire. All the children were involved, and Jack decided that he would make some buttons for the robot. At this point the model was lying across the workshop table, so he started sticking plastic lids of different colours down the centre. As he worked, he was talking to himself – 'If you press this one he will light up, and this one will make him talk.' At this point the Deputy Head walked in and wandered over to him. She watched for a minute, then pointed to a button and said, 'What colour is this one?' Jack looked at her completely blankly for a second and then told her. She could then mentally tick a box. What had she missed?

It's necessary that we believe that the child is very intelligent, that the child is strong and beautiful and has very ambitious desires and requests. This is the image of the child that we need to hold.
(Malaguzzi, 1993)

CONCLUSION – SO, DO I THINK MY METHODS WORK?

The Deputy Head in the story of Jack is, of course, the same one that asked me the question that forms the title of this chapter. Well, obviously I do think they work, and I have built on and developed my approach over the years. But what gives me the right to say this? The story of Jack is one of many examples in my practice which, even before my research degrees, showed me that studying and reflecting – 'action research' – is important. It's about what is happening now, not what is happening next. Meaningful, purposeful results for the children and the adults. Remember that your practice will not be the same year after year, and it should not be. This will not be an easy journey, but the more informed you are the more you will be able to successfully demonstrate a 'Pedagogical Approach'. I will finish with the definition of this from Getting it Right in the Early Years Foundation Stage:

> Pedagogic Approach: Pedagogy refers to educative interactions between teachers, children, parents. It also includes how teaching and learning are shaped by the learning environment and the learning tasks offered within this. The broad term includes how teachers, parents and children relate together as well as the teaching approaches implemented. It also has reference to the wider community and family context in which the child and the adults in their world are operating. (British Association for Early Childhood Education, 2019)

All this requires research.

Top tips

- Always make sure to read things that may run contrary to your philosophy. But beware of fads and fashions. These are research of a sort, but not always from a respected source. Social media can be a minefield.
- Keep an open mind and keep reflecting on something – research is about the 'why', not the 'what works'. Any outcome may take a long time to show.
- Be prepared to think 'out of the box' – it's about 'what now', not 'what next'.

REFERENCES

Archer, N. (2020). Dictated by data? Retrieved from www.earlyyearseducator.co.uk/features/article/dictated-by-data.

DfE (2017/2020). Statutory Framework for the Early Years Foundation Stage: Setting the standards for learning, development and care for children from birth to five. July 2020 version.

Malaguzzi, L. (1993). Your image of the child: Where teaching begins. Comments translated and adapted from a seminar presented by Professor Loris Malaguzzi in Reggio Emilia, Italy, June 1993. Retrieved from https://www.reggioalliance.org/downloads/malaguzzi:ccie:1994.pdf.

Novella, S. (2008). Brain Gym – This is your brain on pseudoscience. Retrieved from https://theness.com/neurologicablog/index.php/brain-gym-this-is-your-brain-on-pseudoscience/.

Oxford English Dictionary. (Tablet/phone app version)

Pascal, C., Bertram, T. and Rouse, L. (2019). Getting it right in the Early Years Foundation Stage: a review of the evidence. British Association for Early Childhood Education (Early Education). Retrieved from https://www.early-education.org.uk/sites/default/files/Getting%20it%20right%20in%20the%20EYFS%20Literature%20Review.pdf.

Tickell, C. (2011). The Early Years: Foundations for life, health and learning – An Independent Report on the Early Years Foundation Stage to Her Majesty's Government. Retrieved from https://assets.publishing.service.gov.uk/government/uploads/system/uploads/attachment_data/file/180919/DFE-00177-2011.pdf.

IMPROVING PRE-SCHOOL EDUCATION WITH ACTION RESEARCH

KRISTINA WESTLUND

Kristina Westlund is a research and development leader in the City of Malmö, Sweden. She supports research-based school improvement in the municipality, with a special interest in Early Childhood Education and Care. Kristina has previously worked as a pre-school teacher.

The Swedish Education Act stipulates that all education in Sweden must be based on science and proven experience. In other words, both teaching methods and learning content must be based on best available knowledge. Teachers must be able to make use of relevant results from research and combine that knowledge with the experiences that have been aggregated over time by the teacher community. This chapter will provide a description of how an action research framework could be used for improving pre-school education, with examples from Swedish pre-schools.

PRE-SCHOOL IN SWEDEN

In Sweden children attend pre-school between the ages of one and five. The year they turn six, compulsory school starts with one year of pre-school class before they begin Grade 1 aged seven. The Swedish pre-school is a full-day service, where education and care are integrated throughout the whole day. A national curriculum has been in place since 1998 (Skolverket, 2018), and this applies to all children in pre-school, regardless of age. There are no learning goals that children are assessed by, but there are goals regarding the learning opportunities that pre-schools must provide. Teaching in pre-school should be based on what the children show an interest in and their previous experiences, combined with the learning content specified in the national curriculum.

In the last revision of the curriculum (Skolverket, 2018), the concept of teaching was introduced. In Sweden pre-school has been classified as school since the 2011 Education Act (and has been governed by the Ministry of Education since 1998). But in 2018 the responsibility of the pre-school teacher in 'teaching' was included in the curriculum for the first time. A report from the Swedish School Inspectorate (Skolinspektionen, 2016) criticised pre-school teachers for not considering themselves to be 'teaching' the children. This can be understood in relation to the strong tradition of *educare* and holistic, play-based learning in Swedish pre-schools (Eidevald et al., 2018). Pre-school teachers feared that using the term 'teaching' in pre-school would draw thinking towards formal teaching, where teachers were supposed to 'transfer' knowledge to the children. The dominant view of learning in pre-school has been that learning can take place all the time through children's own initiatives, with the right adult guidance. The criticism of this dominant view was that teachers' actions – teaching – became invisible (Skolinspektionen, 2016). By introducing the concept of teaching for pre-school in the national curriculum, the National Agency of Education initiated a nationwide discussion of what implications this could have for pre-school education. Many pre-school teachers started to search for best available knowledge on how to understand 'teaching' in their context.

A PRE-SCHOOL EDUCATION BASED ON SCIENCE AND PROVEN EXPERIENCE

As mentioned earlier, all education in Sweden must be based on science and proven experience. The National Agency of Education in Sweden recently published a report on this subject, entitled 'Asking questions and looking for answers' (Skolverket, 2020). The title itself provides a clear indication of what is expected from a research-based education. There has been a shift of perspective in how the use of research in education is described. From mainly focusing on how to implement research results in practice, where teachers could be regarded as recipients, teachers are now expected to be active in asking questions and looking for answers. Research (results and methods) can then be viewed as a tool for teachers in constructing their professional knowledge base. Collaboration and structure are important aspects, according to the aforementioned publication. The importance of research literacy is also pointed out. Research literacy, as defined by the National Agency of Education, is to have a basic understanding of research and of how results from research can be used to improve education. For example, by having some understanding of scientific frameworks and research methodology, teachers can assess what contribution to knowledge different studies provide and whether the results could be useful in relation to their own teaching. Persson (2017) describes research literacy as being able to understand, assess and use research. He underlines the importance of teachers themselves being the ones who need to decide which results from research are relevant for them. Persson also points to the difference between research *on* teachers and research *with* teachers. Both can be useful and relevant for teachers, but when teachers are included in the research process, they are involved in defining aims and research questions.

BENEFITS OF INVOLVING TEACHERS IN RESEARCHING THEIR OWN PRACTICE

Within the framework of action research, researching *with* practitioners is an important foundation. Action research includes many different strands, but one common aim is the collaboration between researchers and practitioners. The production of new knowledge is closely related to changing practice. By changing practice, practitioners also develop their understanding of the practice (Rönnerman, 2003). In Sweden Professor Karin Rönnerman has made an important contribution to the use of action research as a method for improving pre-school education (Rönnerman, 2003; Nylund et al., 2010). The dual components of action research – action and research – are crucial for understanding how this approach could be useful for improving pre-school education. *Action* is about trying something new, introducing a different way of working. *Research* is about systematically collecting data during the process and using theory for analysing the results and drawing conclusions. Rönnerman's orientation within the action research framework is towards the critical participatory action research (cf. Kemmis and McTaggart, 2005). She points out the risk of action research becoming a technical tool for professional development. There is an emancipatory potential in involving teachers in researching their own practice (Nylund et al., 2010). The (research) work of researchers has traditionally been viewed as more important than the work of teachers. The language used by researchers often creates a barrier that makes it difficult for teachers to understand and use the research. Teachers are thereby put in a position where their experience-based, context-specific knowledge is regarded as being of less importance than the academic, generalised knowledge of researchers. Involving teachers in research is important for strengthening their professional knowledge base (Nias, 1991). Teachers need to make their knowledge public and share it with colleagues. Only then can the professional knowledge be accumulated and verified by a larger number of teachers over time, which is a central part of building a shared professional knowledge base (Hiebert et al., 2002).

EXPLORING 'TEACHING' IN PRE-SCHOOL THROUGH ACTION RESEARCH

The arguments for involving teachers in researching practice, combined with building and sharing professional knowledge, is aligned with the ambition of a pre-school education based on science and proven experience. There is also a connection to research literacy, and the idea that the ability to understand, assess and use research will contribute to the professionalisation of pre-school teachers (Persson, 2017).

Using action research as a framework for exploring the concept of teaching in pre-school education has been a way to contribute to a professional language and an understanding of teaching that is grounded in practice as well as in theory. From the point of view of many pre-school teachers, the term 'teaching' has mainly been used to describe the work of teachers within the compulsory school system. As mentioned before, there was a certain fear that using this concept would lead to a 'schoolification' of pre-school education. There was an obvious need for teachers to create their own understanding of what a teaching practice in pre-school could look like, based on research and experience. Even though there are no learning goals for children in Swedish pre-schools, the Swedish Schools Inspectorate (Skolinspektionen, 2016) defined teaching as 'goal-oriented', meaning that it is not enough to support children in learning activities of their own choice. The learning content of the national curriculum must therefore be in focus. Pre-school teachers have a responsibility to challenge and stimulate the children's learning and development towards the goals in the curriculum.

Instead of simply importing the concept of teaching from another part of the school system, researching how teaching could be understood in pre-school education has the potential to empower pre-school teachers and strengthen their professional knowledge.

USING THE STEPS OF ACTION RESEARCH IN A CONTEXT OF PRE-SCHOOL IMPROVEMENT

There are different ways to describe the process of action research, but one way is to include the following steps: *plan – act & observe – reflect – revised plan –* and then continue like a spiral (Kemmis and McTaggart, 2005). Every attempt to illustrate a complex process with a simple visual model will necessarily reduce the significance of moving back and forward between the steps. In addition, there is always a need to adapt the process of each step depending on the specific context. In a pre-school where the teachers are used to reading research and systematically studying their own work, the process will be conducted differently than it will in a pre-school where research literacy is at a beginner stage.

In this chapter, a description will be given of how the action research process has been used in the specific context of exploring the concept of teaching in four pre-schools in Malmö, Sweden, and what have appeared to be crucial aspects – and challenges – within each step. The work of a pre-school teacher who participated in the process, studying her own teaching of mathematics through play, will be used as illustration. Her work is in many ways representative of the process of most of the participating teachers, and it has been chosen for illustration both because it clearly shows what she learned from observing her own teaching and because it shows how the use of different theories makes it possible to understand different aspects of the practice.

Plan

Making a plan might sound like the easy part, but this has shown itself to be a step where the teachers have put in a significant amount of work. In planning the process, the teachers need to identify their research problem, choose a research question and plan what action they want to try in order to improve their teaching. They also need to make a plan of which methods they want to use for data collection. In some cases, this step has taken a year or more.

One fundamental challenge affecting the whole process is to identify a topic that is relevant for the teachers. The questions they ask need to be genuine and meaningful for their work. In Swedish pre-schools, the amount of time the teachers have for work outside the classroom is limited to a few hours per week, which makes it necessary that all improvement work must be perceived as meaningful. The research problem should be connected to the actual needs and challenges that the teachers face in their daily work. It is also important to include the whole work team. All the pre-school teachers have used mind maps to identify which aspects of teaching they want to focus on. The next step has been to connect their choice of focus to a curriculum goal.

The reason this might be difficult is that most documentation that is traditionally carried out in pre-schools is used for *describing* the education, not *studying* it. Pre-school teachers document their work for communication with parents or to report their systematic quality work to the central organisation of the municipality. This kind of documentation focuses on what is known; but when they use the action research process to explore the concept of teaching, they are expected to focus on what is unknown. Before getting used to this change of perspective, there is a tendency to choose to study something where the answer is already known. This may lead to a documentation of teaching methods that the teachers know will work well in their context. The construction of new knowledge will be limited, and the teachers will perceive the process as a burden – something that is expected from them in addition to all the other things they need to do. In the planning step, the teachers have been asked to argue why there is a need to study the topic they have chosen. What is the knowledge gap? Once the teachers find their own curiosity in the process, they don't need to question the relevance of studying their work.

Early in the process, all pre-school teachers in the participating pre-schools have read and discussed research on teaching in pre-school. It has helped them to identify knowledge gaps as well as to come up with ideas about how to act to improve their own teaching. They have also read literature about methodology, which has been helpful to identify possible ways to study their practice.

One of the participating teachers chose to study her teaching of mathematics, related to this goal from the curriculum: 'The pre-school should provide each child with the conditions to develop an ability to discern, express, investigate and use mathematical concepts and their interrelationships' (Skolverket, 2018, p. 14). Her aim was to better understand the teaching of mathematics which took place at an outdoor 'grocery store' that the teachers and children had built together. The purpose of the store itself was multiple – to increase the level of children's participation and to offer conditions for playful learning, construction, aesthetical learning processes, etc. But the research question was narrowed down to focus on the teaching of mathematics. This is an example of another challenge for teachers studying their own practice. As Nias (1991) pointed out, the practical knowledge of teachers is context specific, which can make it difficult to separate different phenomena from each other. But the narrowing down is important if it is to be possible to answer the questions.

Act & observe

Once the planning phase is done, it is time to carry out the action part of the process. In reality, this might be a step where teachers need to go back and revise their plan. For example, after planning which methods to use for data collection during the process, teachers might need to try to identify if the methods are suitable for answering the questions they are asking. In this step, it has been helpful to use the group for collective analysis. What becomes visible for other colleagues in the group? Do the tools for documentation register the data needed for analysis? Observing the act of teaching was often a challenge for the teachers. Traditionally, most documentation in pre-school focuses on the actions of children, not teachers. The teachers are more comfortable using documentation to identify the process of learning than the process of teaching. Since the concept of teaching was vague for many of the teachers, it became difficult to identify how teaching should be documented. What should they look for? With the purpose of studying teaching, it was decided that all teachers should use video recordings as a tool for observation. This made it easier to collectively study teaching strategies in different situations.

The teacher who studied her teaching of mathematics at the outdoor 'grocery store' asked a colleague to record her interactions with the children. The activities at the store were arranged around buying and selling groceries, which was a playful activity where children chose whether or not to participate. Teachers were always present at the store to support the children. All children would have a wallet with 10 pearls for shopping, each pearl representing a Swedish krona (SEK). They always received a receipt specifying what they had bought. The receipt included illustrations of the groceries and a calculation of the costs.

The initial observations showed that the children seemed to have a good understanding of the calculations that were done and of the fact that the number of pearls represented a sum of money. The teacher planned her action to explore how her teaching could stimulate the children's understanding of mathematical concepts and relations. She decided to offer a variety of coins that they created together out of wood. But now the coins could represent different sums of money between 1 and 5 SEK. The wallets would still contain 'money' of the value of 10 SEK. Her colleagues continued to make video observations of her interaction with the children at the store.

Reflect

A lot of time and effort have been spent on collectively analysing the video material. There is always a risk of being too quick in drawing conclusions. Teachers' practical knowledge makes them experts on finding solutions in the moment, but in the reflection phase of the action research process they have been challenged to study the situation from different perspectives. The video observations have been approached in three steps – description, interpretation and analysis. Describing is often the most difficult part – just concentrating on what information is given from the film sequence. To make a reliable analysis, it is important not to mix interpretations of data with one's own preconceptions (in other words, to remain open-minded).

In the example with the grocery store, the teacher studied the consequences of her decision to offer coins of different values. Many children still chose the 'old' wallets with 10 pearls, which were still available. The children who chose the new coins often looked for items in the store with the exact price that the coins represented. The teacher studied how she supported the children's problem-solving in order to understand her own teaching strategies and to find ways to create better conditions for mathematical learning in the activity. The results were analysed from a perspective of variation theory (Björklund and Pramling Samuelsson, 2018). With support from this theory, which highlights how variation and perspectives can create conditions for learning by distinguishing phenomena from each other, the teacher could develop new strategies and improve her teaching. Over time, she observed how the children's understanding of mathematical relations increased, and how some children even started to write their own receipts. She also observed how the playful activity enabled teaching that attracted and supported children aged between two and five simultaneously. Between observations, she revised her teaching acts based on the findings and the use of theory. This represents the 'last' step of the action research process, *revised plan*, which will not be outlined in any detail here.

The group of teachers have been continually reading and reflecting on literature together, about both methodology and theories on teaching in pre-school. The strength of conducting the reflection phase in a group is that different perspectives can be added to each other, challenging pre-existing assumptions about the object of study (in this case, teaching). When video recordings of activities at the grocery store were analysed, other teachers included relational aspects in the analysis. While the teacher in focus was mainly concentrating on her use of mathematical concepts and reasoning, her colleagues noted body language and tone of voice, which initiated a discussion on what characterises teaching in the playful and care-related context of pre-school education. When using a different theory in the analysis, teaching could be understood from another perspective. The theory of pedagogical relations, with social, cognitive and emotional support as analytical tools (Persson, 2019), made other aspects of teaching more visible than the variation theory did.

CONCLUSION

Changing practice, according to Kemmis et al. (2014), is to change the way we talk about the practice (sayings), the actions within the practice (doings) and the distribution of power connected to that practice (relatings). All three aspects have been important in the process of exploring the concept of teaching in pre-school education. The collective reading and analysis have contributed to developing the way of talking about teaching in pre-school. The teachers became more comfortable talking about their work in terms of teaching. The action research process has helped them focus on improving the act of teaching. Video observation was an effective tool to identify teaching strategies – even the smallest ones, which sometimes turn out to be the most important. And finally, the collective process of reflection has helped to develop the professional knowledge and understanding of teaching in pre-school. It has also helped in connecting research-based knowledge to experience-based knowledge, strengthening the research literacy of the teachers. This makes the teachers more confident in their profession as pre-school teachers. There is no longer any need to fear that the concept of teaching will lead to abandoning the pre-school tradition of integrating play, education and care.

TOP TIPS

- Keep it simple! A well-defined research question and selection of situations for observation help the teachers handle and make sense of the action research process.
- Choose relevant topics! By connecting the process to topics that engage teachers and make them curious, the use of research will not be perceived as 'one more thing that must be done'. It will instead be a welcome source of knowledge.
- The use of video observations has enabled different perspectives and perceptions in a way that can be difficult using other methods. It is especially useful in a group of teachers who wish to become more familiar with analysing their work.

REFERENCES
Björklund, C. and Pramling Samuelsson, I. (2018). Undervisning, lek, lärande och omsorg – förskolans hörnstenar [Teaching, playing, learning and caring – the cornerstones of the preschool]. In S. Sheridan and P. Williams, *Undervisning i förskolan: En kunskapsöversikt [Teaching in preschool: An overview of knowledge]*. Stockholm: Skolverket.

Eidevald, C., Engdahl, I., Frankenberg, S., Lenz Taguchi, H. and Palmer, A. (2018). Omsorgsfull och lekfull utbildning och undervisning i förskolan [Careful and playful education and teaching in preschool]. In S. Sheridan and P. Williams, *Undervisning i förskolan: En kunskapsöversikt [Teaching in preschool: An overview of knowledge]*. Stockholm: Skolverket.

Hiebert, J., Gallimore, R. and Stigler, J. W. (2002). A knowledge base for the teaching profession: What would it look like and how can we get one?, *Educational Researcher* 31(5), 3–15.

Kemmis, S. and McTaggart, R. (2005). Participatory action research: Communicative action and the public sphere. In N. K. Denzin and Y. S. Lincoln (eds), *The Sage handbook of qualitative research* (pp. 559–603). Thousand Oaks, CA: Sage Publications Ltd.

Kemmis, S., Wilkinson, J., Edwards-Groves, C., Hardy, I. and Grootenboer, P. (2014). *Changing practices, changing education.* New York, NY: Springer.

Nias, J. (1991). How practitioners are silenced, how practitioners are empowered. In H. K. Letiche, J. C. Van Der Wolf and F. X. Plooij (eds). *The practitioner's power of choice in staff-development and in-service training* (pp. 19–36). Amsterdam: Swets & Zeitlinger.

Nylund, M., Sandback, C., Wilhelmsson, B. and Rönnerman, K. (2010). *Aktionsforskning i förskolan – trots att schemat är fullt [Action research in pre-school – despite a full schedule].* Stockholm: Lärarförbundets förlag.

Persson, S. (2017). *Forskningslitteracitet: En introduktion till att förstå, värdera och använda vetenskaplig kunskap [Research literacy: An introduction to understanding, assessing and using scientific knowledge].* Forskning i korthet nr 1 2017. Kommunförbundet Skåne.

Persson, S. (2019). Pedagogiska relationer och det professionella subjektet [Pedagogical relations and the professional subject]. In P. Dahlbeck and K. Westlund (eds). *Relationell pedagogik – i teori och praktik i förskolan [Relational education – in theory and practice of the pre-school].* Lund: Studentlitteratur.

Rönnerman, K. (2003). Action research: Educational tools and the improvement of practice, *Educational Action Research* 11(1), 9–22.

Skolinspektionen (2016). Förskolans kvalitet och måluppfyllelse 2015–2017. Delrapport 1 [Preschool quality and goal achievement 2015-2017. Sub-report 1]. Dnr: 2015:3 364. Available at: www.skolinspektionen.se.

Skolverket (2018). Lpfö 18. Curriculum for the pre-school. Available at: www.skolverket.se.

Skolverket (2020). Att ställa frågor och söka svar: Samarbete för vetenskaplig grund och beprövad erfarenhet [Asking questions and looking for answers: Collaboration for a scientific basis and proven experience]. Stockholm: Skolverket.

RESEARCH-INFORMED TEACHER, LEADER AND LEARNER

KATIE STEARS

Katie Sears is currently a Lead Teacher of Inclusion, Teaching and Learning and class teacher at a five-form primary called Sha Tin Junior School, which is in Hong Kong. For the past nine years she has taught in Hong Kong as a mainstream and learning support class teacher, as well as a specialist teacher of Information & Digital Literacies. Prior to this, she taught at two primary schools in England. During this time, she had a number of roles, including Assistant Head, Key Stage 1 Leader and Early Years Foundation Stage Leader. The vast majority of her teaching experience has been with the Early Years/Lower Primary age range (four to seven years). She taught the English National Curriculum and Early Years Foundation Stage whilst in England and now follows the IB PYP (International Baccalaureate Primary Years Programme).

INTRODUCTION

In this chapter I will begin by sharing a little about my educational journey and ethos and the reason why I am a lifelong learner and love to engage in research-informed teaching. Next, I will share two pieces of action research that I have engaged in. The first is an example of research-informed teaching that I have been participating in since 2017. I will outline how Alfie Kohn's (1999) book in particular, plus wider reading around the impact of intrinsic and extrinsic rewards, has affected my classroom practice. The other piece of research-informed teaching that I will discuss is the rapid move to online teaching and learning that was necessary in 2020 as a result of the closure of school buildings during the COVID-19 pandemic. Finally, in the conclusion I will share some suggestions that could be adopted by those interested in engaging in research-informed teaching.

LIFELONG LEARNER – KNOW BETTER, DO BETTER!

I have seen the phrase 'lifelong learner' used in a variety of biographies and it is widely used in PYP/inquiry-based schools. I personally align very strongly with this disposition. After completing my Postgraduate Certificate in Education (PGCE) in Primary Education (2003) and gaining my first teaching position, I felt there was still so much for me to learn. In my second to fourth years of teaching I completed a Master's in Education. Working full-time and using my weekends and holidays for reading and essay writing was a time-consuming activity but something that I loved. It definitely awakened a desire within me to continue seeking out new learning opportunities.

I have been fortunate to have had the opportunity to attend presentations by a variety of well-recognised educational thinkers throughout my teaching career, including Pie Corbett, Shirley Clarke, Kath Murdoch, Dylan Wiliam, Ron Ritchhart, Pam Hook and many more great educators. In addition, I have continually focused on my professional development by reading books or articles, watching or listening to podcasts or engaging in social media – Twitter or Facebook.

As a full-time teacher and mum of two, I try to balance my work and home life somewhat, but for a reflective educator who is constantly wanting to learn more, this is a challenge! During term time I typically listen to podcasts while commuting (a particular favourite of mine is Education Bookcast by Pstrokonski) or read shorter articles or my Twitter feed. I often use my holidays to set aside time to focus on a more time-consuming aspect of professional development, such as reading a full book or preparing a presentation. For instance, I am writing this chapter during the Christmas holidays of 2020!

Each time I learn a new piece of information, I reflect on the relevance to my current role and school-based responsibilities. The focus of what I am considering is broad at times, and I might simultaneously be considering a variety of areas linked to education. At other moments I might have a much more targeted or specific goal or area in mind. For instance, at the moment I have three main areas that I am considering to a greater or lesser extent. Firstly, I currently have responsibility for Digital Citizenship in my school, so this is something I have on my radar. Secondly, the schools in Hong Kong have returned to online learning, so I am keeping an eye out for activities, apps or engagements to use with my own class. Thirdly, I am four years into an action research project into the use of intrinsic motivation/reward-free classrooms. Finally, when time permits, I very much enjoy 'seeing what's out there', for example, clicking into articles or ideas raised on my Twitter feed or reading an educational journal or article.

I realise that for some educators this ongoing focus on educational research whilst working full-time might seem to be too onerous or time consuming. However, for me it is something that I am driven to do. I personally find it highly gratifying to engage in professional development and constantly feel the need to 'collect all the pieces of a puzzle' to enable me to be a better practitioner. In fact, I find continual professional development to be somewhat of an obsession for me and I am always thinking, *what more and what next?*

INTRINSIC MOTIVATION/'REWARD-FREE' LEARNING ENVIRONMENT

Over the past few years I have been reconsidering and reflecting on my own use of reward systems. In the past I used a variety of reward systems, for example, stickers, certificates and house points, in order to encourage students to engage and focus on their learning. In 2017 I was a member of the positive education working group within my school. We were rewriting the school's Positive Relationship Policy (formerly called behaviour management policy), with a shift away from traditional behaviour management approaches and a move towards positive education practices, focusing on relationships, student agency and restorative practice. During this period, I came across an article (Flanagan, 2017) that really caused me to reflect and go deeper into the psychology of rewards and think about the impact of extrinsic and intrinsic reward systems.

In the following years I researched more about the work of Alfie Kohn, Daniel Pink and other behavioural theorists/psychologists and learnt more about motivation and rewards. In addition, I considered how Dweck's (2006) work on mindset is enacted within classroom reward systems.

Kohn's (1999) work, in particular, has reverberated with me strongly. I realise that many of his points are related to contingent rewards, and whilst I do not believe that the awarding of stickers/certificates/house points is as harmful as telling a child 'if you do X, then I will give you a sweet', I do nonetheless worry about the message we are giving to students with regard to who is rewarded and what they are rewarded for. Some of the key points from Kohn's book that have resonated with me are:

- 'Rewards are less effective than intrinsic motivation for promoting effective learning' (p. 144).
- 'Controlling environments have been shown consistently to reduce people's interest in whatever they are doing' (p. 140).
- When teachers reward this leads to a lack of autonomy [student autonomy] (p. 154).
- 'Rewards and punishments are worthless at best, and destructive at worst, for helping children develop such values and skills [e.g. social skills]. What words and punishments do produce is *temporary compliance.* They buy us obedience ... Good values have to be grown from the inside out ... No behavioural manipulation ever helped a child develop a commitment to becoming a caring and responsible person.' (p. 161).
- 'Anyone who is rewarded for acts of generosity will be less likely to think of himself as a caring or altruistic person' (p. 173).
- 'Rewards rupture relationships. They open up a huge chasm between the parent and child, now defined as the rewarder and the rewarded' (p. 175).

I was greatly affected by the research I read and felt that I needed to make changes to my teaching based on this. For this reason, for the past three to four years I have been carrying out my own action research. I have not given any extrinsic rewards (stickers, certificates, house points, etc.) within my classroom because I was uncertain about the message I was giving to the students. Instead, I have favoured developing a sense of community, relationship building, student agency and the fostering of intrinsic motivation. I considered how Kohn's three C's – collaboration, content and choice (pp. 214–221) – and Pink's (2011) focus on autonomy, mastery and purpose would translate into a primary learning environment and impact on intrinsic motivation.

For the first couple of years, I was the Information Literacy teacher within the school, so I was carrying out this action research across the whole school, as I taught all 30 classes, aged 4–11, on a regular basis. More recently I have returned to being a classroom teacher and have continued to maintain a 'reward-free' learning environment.

Whilst carrying out this action research, I deepened my knowledge by searching for article titles that linked to the same theme. In particular, I was looking for evidence of how Kohn's research translated into an educational setting and the impact on the students. I read a number of articles that were linked to intrinsic motivation – Selart et al. (2008), Pierce et al. (2003), Reineke et al. (2008) and Marinak and Gambrell (2008). Most relevant to Early Years was the work of Ulber et al. (2016), who researched three-year-olds and found that children would try to equalise unfair resource distribution in the absence of any reinforcement or authority, but that those who had been given a material incentive for sharing later refused to share when the rewarding had stopped. I also looked at some articles/newspaper reports on schools that have become 'reward-free' schools.

Whilst I have not tracked or studied the data from my action research in a formal way, I have drawn some general conclusions based on my observations of the students. I have also reflected on my own practice and noted a shift in my dialogue with the students. This was a small-scale study, so I don't seek to make any broad claims. From my personal perspective, I embarked on this research wondering what it would be like to teach in a reward-free learning environment. Whilst it hasn't always been straightforward – the most challenging time was probably the first month of teaching a new class that was used to a learning environment with frequent external rewards offered – I have stayed true to my goal of doing what I believe is ultimately in the best interest of the students. Yes, they like stickers, certificates, etc., but ultimately they might come to rely on these to the detriment of intrinsic motivation. I have also found it to be quite a freeing experience to focus on learning conversations with the students without having to manage a variety of external rewards. For instance, when I dialogue with a student about their learning, we discuss what went well and what could be improved without having to then give an external reward that could actually detract from the learning focus. I feel this also aligns with Dweck's notion of growth mindset.

Whilst I don't feel that I have sufficient evidence to conclusively say that rewards are 'bad' (in fact I would like to study this area further), it does seem to me – based on the research I have done as well as my own experiences – that giving rewards can be problematic, whereas giving no rewards does not negatively impact student learning/behaviour and in many ways seems to be advantageous. Primarily, the impact has been within my own classroom. On a wider school level – within my year level – I introduced a student celebratory certificate that was completed by students to recognise something they were proud of (rather than a certificate given by a teacher). In addition, on a school-wide basis the teachers who were using contingent rewards (e.g. if you get 50 house points you can eat popcorn) are no longer using this approach. I would like to extend my ideas further across the school but have not yet had the opportunity to do so.

REMOTE LEARNING – 2020 GLOBAL PANDEMIC

When we heard in February 2020 that schools in Hong Kong would be closed because of a coronavirus, I found the shift to remote/online learning to be a dramatic change from the face-to-face Early Years classroom environment I had taken for granted for so many years. I felt a heightened need to reach out to international educators to learn more about how other schools were adapting to the new way of teaching. As a regular user of Twitter, I immediately began to seek out other educators who were in a similar position. When I saw that the whole international community was looking for answers, I realised that many educators were also seeking advice. At this point I changed tack, and so in addition to looking to learn from others I also realised that my own digital expertise would enable me to share my practice with others. Therefore, I tweeted on a regular basis throughout the beginning of 2020 about lessons I had developed in an online context, apps I felt would be advantageous to use, the differentiation of learning through the use of SOLO taxonomy, plus a variety of other tips. As a result of this sharing, I was invited to join a podcast discussion, 'Virtual School Roundtable', for the Special Educational Network and Inclusion Association (Boll, Mejia and Stears, 2020).

I attended numerous webinars during this period in order to better understand the remote learning environment. I also collaborated with colleagues within my own school as well as international educators via Twitter. I kept a record of my learning on a padlet: bit.ly/remotelearningpyp. This kept a track of my professional learning during this period and was also a source of information that I could share with other educators. Through networking with IB educators, I became aware that there was a need for Early Years/Lower Primary teachers to come together to discuss and share ideas about this new way of teaching and learning. Therefore, in April 2020 I facilitated a discussion that collaboratively inquired into the question, 'What does remote learning look like in the Early Years/Lower Primary/PYP class?' This virtual discussion (Stears, 2020) was attended by around a hundred international educators and I was delighted that Kath Murdoch, a guru of inquiry-based learning, also joined the conversation. In May I was invited to join a panel discussion hosted by Highr/FICCI ARISE (Federation of Indian Chambers of Commerce and Industry/Alliance for Re-Imagining School Education), which addressed the question of 'Managing Student Engagement Online' (2020). On this occasion, more than a thousand attendees joined to learn about teaching in a virtual environment.

During the first half of 2020, I was working full-time in the intense and unknown environment of remote/online learning. The dual motivators for me during this time were to upskill and inform myself about effective online teaching and learning whilst sharing with my fellow global educators. Being a research-informed teacher at this point was vital for me so that I could swiftly adapt to the new teaching approaches and reflect upon best practices in the online learning context.

CONCLUSION

Based on my own experiences, I will now make some suggestions for how educators who wish to engage in research-informed teaching could begin. Firstly, I would suggest that educators are open-minded to new ideas/approaches and seek out learning beyond their own school/setting. 'You don't know what you don't know', so I would recommend starting by looking into one (or more) of the options listed below. When reading or listening, you could either view with a specific interest area in mind or simply see what might spark your interest. Options could be:

- reading articles on the TES (*Times Educational Supplement*) or online sources such as Mindshift (https://www.kqed.org/mindshift)
- educational journals – I would recommend joining the Chartered College of Teaching (https://chartered.college/join/) for low-cost access to a quality educational and research database
- viewing/listening to a blog, vlog or podcast (Education Bookcast ttps://educationbookcast.libsyn.com/ is a particular favourite)
- engaging in social media, for instance, using hashtags in Twitter (e.g. #earlyyears) and building a PLN (professional learning network) of colleagues whom you follow and exchange ideas with (if you wish, please connect with me via Twitter, see @stearskatie).

Secondly, I would encourage you to be brave and go for it once you find an area of research that is interesting to you! Sometimes making small tweaks to your practice can make a big difference, but, if you try something and find it doesn't work for you/your context, then view that as a positive learning process too. Obviously, you have to be careful that any changes you make do not have a negative impact on student learning, but if you evaluate and reflect throughout the process, then hopefully you will be aware if this turns out to be the case. Also, don't be afraid to be the only one in your school/setting who is trialling a new approach. For example, last year my classroom was the only 'shoe-free' learning environment in my school. Support from the leadership team is helpful to enable you to make whole-school changes. On the other hand, there are many tweaks that you can make within your own learning environment.

Finally, if you learn about a new approach or piece of research, or you have personal experiences, I would encourage you to share them. The more we can connect and learn from each other the better, in my opinion.

TOP TIPS

In summary, my three suggestions for anyone who is interested in becoming a research-informed teacher are:

- Look beyond your school or setting.
- Be brave and go for it!
- Share about what you learn.

REFERENCES

Boll, L., Mejia, K. and Stears, K. (2020). SENIA Virtual School Roundtable, Special Educational Network and Inclusion Association (SENIA). Retrieved from https://seniainternational.org/senia-virtual-school-roundtable/.

Dweck, C. (2006). *Mindset: The new psychology of success.* New York, NY: Ballantine Books.

Flanagan, L. (2017). How a school ditched awards and assemblies to refocus on kids and learning', KQED. Retrieved from https://www.kqed.org/mindshift/48745/how-a-school-ditched-awards-and-assemblies-to-refocus-on-kids-and-learning.

Highr/FICCI ARISE (Federation of Indian Chambers of Commerce and Industry/Alliance for Re-Imagining School Education) (2020). Managing student engagement online. Retrieved from https://fb.watch/2xD2UKi5Kp/.

Kohn, A. (1999). *Punished by rewards: The trouble with gold stars, incentive plans, A's, praise, and other bribes.* Boston, MA and New York, NY: Mariner Books.

Marinak, B. A. and Gambrell, L. B. (2008). Intrinsic Motivation and Rewards: What Sustains Young Children's Engagement with Text?, *Literacy Research and Instruction* 47(1), 9–26. Retrieved from https://eric.ed.gov/?id=EJ811774

Pierce, W., Cameron, J., Banko, K. and So, S. (2003). Positive effects of rewards and performance standards on intrinsic motivation, *The Psychological Record* 53, 561–579.

Pink, D. (2011). *Drive: The surprising truth about what motivates us.* New York, NY: Riverhead Books.

Pstrokonski, S. Education Bookcast. Retrieved from https://educationbookcast. libsyn.com/.

Reineke, J., Sonsteng, K. and Gartrell, D. (2008). Nurturing mastery motivation: No need for rewards, *Young Children* 63(6), 93–97.

Selart, M., Nordstrom, T., Kuvaas, B. and Takemura, K. (2008). Effects of reward on self-regulation, intrinsic motivation and creativity', *Scandinavian Journal of Educational Research* 52(5), 439–458.

Stears, K., 2020. What does remote learning look like in the Early Years/Lower Primary/PYP class?' IB Educators Chats. Retrieved from https://sites.google. com/view/ib-educators-chat/home?authuser=0.

Ulber, J., Hamaan, K. and Tomasello, M. (2016). Extrinsic rewards diminish costly sharing in 3-year-olds, *Child Development* 87(4), 1192–1203.

THE CURIOUS RESEARCH OF DAVID IN THE EARLY YEARS

DAVID WRIGHT

Following a 25-year career in IT, David retrained in 2004, qualifying as an Early Years teacher, joining his wife Anna as owner of Paint Pots Nursery group comprising day care, pre-school and out-of-school care settings located in the Southampton area. David is currently the national representative for England to the World Forum on Early Childhood Education. Among many roles, David is an author, broadcaster, speaker, commentator, consultant, adviser and trainer. He is an advocate and active campaigner for men in Early Years. His book *Men in Early Years Settings*, co-authored with Dr Simon Brownlow, was awarded Silver category at the national Nursery World Awards in 2019.

I have always been inquisitive and easily distracted. This, of course, means that I find it hard to settle to a task and concentrate long enough to complete it – think missed deadlines. On the other hand, my curiosity and insatiable personal quest for knowledge, coupled with the liberating democracy of the internet, has provided me with seemingly limitless sources of information. Access to the work of people with important and life-changing things to say, and opportunities to develop my understanding of what it means to be human, have not just changed my own outlook, practice and life philosophy. I also feel impelled to pass on what I have discovered in the hope that it will make a positive difference to others' teaching and ultimately to the learning experience and life trajectories of children.

I have no interest in research that has nothing to contribute to the real world of human interaction. For me, research, like good art, must provoke us by challenging our thinking. We should be moved by it intellectually and emotionally to expand our knowledge and evolve our moral stance to become more confident in our pedagogy and advocacy. We need to be able to stand up for our values and to defend what we do and why we do it. Equally, we need to be clear in our thinking and justification for what we will not do. I believe passionately that to be effective educators we must believe in ourselves but at the same time be open to continuous personal development, that is, to research as widely as possible to either validate or challenge our beliefs, to learn new things about the world and ourselves, to grow in our understanding and to adapt our behaviour accordingly. Every day is a learning opportunity.

Research takes many forms. It may be a narrow focus on a specific subject area, but in a wider sense it can also be the establishment of a network that enables us to expose ourselves to the ideas and examples of others. The wider the network, the greater the opportunity for opening ourselves to new influences and attitudes. Here is the challenge, for while we can now build global connections and read and hear from colleagues, experts and commentators on a vast range of subjects on an increasing number of media platforms, we have limited time in which to do so. Discernment is key. We need to establish what is relevant, credible, based in fact and good science and helpful. We need to establish purpose and rigour in our research, narrowing in on helpful lines of enquiry from the morass of data. We need to ask ourselves, 'What can I learn from this and how can I apply it in my context?' Research without application becomes academic study for its own end. Some of us may enjoy this as an intellectual pursuit, but for me it represents a self-serving objective that benefits no one except the researcher. It will not change the world or indeed the world of those within our sphere of influence.

My personal research journey as an educator of children aged 0–5 years, and as a father myself, has followed a linked path from an initial inquisitiveness (based on what I have experienced and observed working directly with children and the limited underpinning knowledge I had) which has developed as I have both increased my awareness of research, theory and knowledge and developed my network of contacts of those working in this field. I had become increasingly interested in child development, the needs and capabilities of very young children and the history of theorists in this field. In particular, I was fascinated by the notion of attachment and the primacy of connection as a human need. Formal child development training had touched on the work of Bowlby, Robertson and Ainsworth, but this was at a superficial level. I knew the term attachment and the types of attachment, but that was about it. Subsequently, I read *Why love matters* by Sue Gerhardt and found that it switched on a metaphorical light. I started to understand, for the first time, how children's emotional welfare and physiological welfare are directly affected by our reactions and responses to their needs and demands.

Subsequent attendance at seminars – hearing from Stuart Shanker speaking on self-regulation (https://self-reg.ca/) ('There is no such thing as a bad kid') and Colwyn Trevarthen about his research on the development of proto-cultural intelligence ('I think the ideal companion is a familiar person who really treats the baby with playful human respect'), and learning about Donald Winnicott's pioneering work on holding ('the continuation of reliable holding in terms of the ever-widening circle of family and school and social life') – whetted my appetite for further research. I seemed to become attuned from that time on to any information about meeting the social and emotional needs of children, and there is plenty of material out there, growing every year!

My specific interest in trauma-informed care was sparked by Suzanne Zeedyck. I don't remember exactly when I started following Suzanne on Twitter, or why, but it was around the time she started her organisation, Connected Baby (www.connectedbaby.net). I recall an intriguing tweet calling for hosts (ostensibly, I believe, for locations in Scotland, where she is based) to screen her film *The Connected Baby*. I immediately volunteered and received a DVD. Thus started a monthly series of free community film nights, promoted to parents, health, education and social services professionals and anyone else interested. Screenings featured DVDs graciously provided by Suzanne on the subject of human connection. My research journey was already birthing a desire to disseminate that which I was learning for myself. It seemed to me that, as my knowledge increased, my thinking changed and my practice changed accordingly, there was an accompanying imperative to raise awareness of the truths I was discovering, not to bring challenge in a confrontational or judgemental way but to provide opportunities for others to review what I had learned and to consider its application in their own situation, for the benefit of others. Along with many who have gone before us and those who currently advocate for children's rights across the world, I was forming a determination that we must do that which is beneficial for children and challenge that which is demonstrably not right.

Some time after my initial free film season, Suzanne once again put out a call for hosts to screen a new documentary, *Resilience* (https://kpjrfilms.co/resilience/). I volunteered and received another DVD with accompanying blurb that talked about Adverse Childhood Experiences (ACEs). This was a new concept for me. Hearing from Andars and Felitti – the original ACEs researchers themselves – in this remarkable film, I was amazed to learn that their research dated back to 1995 when they first discovered the link between children's traumatic experiences and poor health and welfare outcomes in later life. At an epidemiological level, the findings are startling, revealing serious public health consequences. The underpinning science and the implications for practice are clear, and yet I knew nothing about it. What became evident was that very few people seemed to be aware of this seminal study either, or if they were, it had been dismissed.

My journey continues, leading me to explore the biology of trauma. Through the writings of Gabor Mate, Bessel Van Der Kolk, Bruce Perry and Nadine Burke Harris, and through Stephen Porges' work on polyvagal theory, I have learned the holistic nature of the human body, the criticality of feeling safe and the significant influence of relationships.

In September 2018, I attended the 'ACE Aware Scotland' conference (http://aceawarescotland.com/conference/) with Nadine Burke Harris as keynote speaker. It was an extraordinary event that built on the Scottish momentum to inform that country about ACEs. I wrote in my feedback that I felt privileged to attend and to carry an ember back down south in the hope that we could start our own fire of awareness. There are two key phrases that inform my work. The first is a quote attributed to Joe Foderaro:

We need to change the fundamental question 'What's wrong with you?' to 'What has happened to you?' (See Bloom, 1994)

The second is from Nadine Burke Harris, who refers to a 'cumulative dose of healing' (Merrill, 2020).

So how has this research translated into practice? Firstly, as leaders of our organisation, we have reimagined our motto of 'Love, Laughter and Learning' as a pyramid in line with Maslow's hierarchy of needs, with Love as the bottom and the largest layer supporting the layer above it, which is Laughter (or playfulness), and with Learning at the top. The clear message is that Learning cannot happen without the underpinning levels. This is covered on Day 1 of our induction. Everyone who joins the organisation understands our values and can explain the significance of this motto.

All of our team have watched *Resilience*. This has been followed up with training focused on the biology of stress, our role as adults, the implications for supporting children, how to build resilience in their lives and the need for understanding, empathy, compassion and kindness.

We have worked on our daily conversations and interactions – how much of our speech is controlling rather than being validating, praising children and building their emotional literacy?

We changed our policy from 'Behaviour Management' to 'Understanding and Supporting Children's Behaviour'. This in itself has shifted the adult to child relationship paradigm. I continue to monitor and challenge the occasional adult outbursts of 'Stop!', 'Get down!', or 'Pre-school, use our indoor voices!'

For some of our team, it has been a challenge to their entrenched beliefs that the adult's role is to manage and control children's behaviour. The realisation that every interaction with a child is an opportunity for a therapeutic moment that over time becomes healing is powerful. We reframe behaviour from being viewed as challenging to being viewed as distressed. Our actions are no longer punitive. We look to help each child self-regulate and to build their awareness of their own emotions and the effects of their behaviours on others.

We have invited our team to always be curious about our children, to ask themselves what has happened/is happening in this child's life. The extension of this is to include the families in our deliberations and non-judgemental discussions.

Overall, we have encouraged our teams to adopt a rights-based view of each child, valuing and respecting them for who they are.

Beyond Paint Pots, we have purchased a lifetime licence to show *Resilience* through our charity, Families First Southampton. We have continued to host our own screenings and worked in partnership with the Local Authority on a programme of events for their teams. Audiences have included designated safeguarding leads and colleagues from the police, schools, children's centre staff, social services and housing and other agencies.

I have been asked to write about my own discoveries and experiences in this area for educational publications and online blogs and to present on much of this material at conferences and training events. I have delivered a training session on what can be learned and applied in educational establishments from Adverse Childhood Experiences to 120 Ofsted inspectors from all phases of education. The dissemination and influence continues. It is humbling to think that my stumbling curiosity at a time when I had little knowledge or experience would lead to such a change in our thinking, the development of partnerships, a passion for awareness raising, a desire to see transformation across our city and our nation, and opportunities to provide leadership and to see research affecting the lives of children each and every day.

TOP TIPS

- Always be curious about everything. Effective research starts with curiosity.
- Keep your mind open with a desire to learn, grow and change. Ask – what can I learn from this? What can I apply from it to my context? How will this yield benefit?
- Be passionate. Carry others with you by being confident in your belief, in the knowledge that underpins this belief and in its efficacy.

REFERENCES

ACE Aware Nation. Retrieved from www.aceawarescotland.com.

Anda, R. F. and Felitti V. J. (1998). Relationship of childhood abuse and household dysfunction to many of the leading causes of death in adults: The Adverse Childhood Experiences (ACE) Study, *American Journal of Preventive Medicine* 14(4), 245–258. Retrieved from https://www.ajpmonline.org/article/S0749-3797(98)00017-8/abstract.

Bloom, S. (1994). The Sanctuary Model: Developing Generic Inpatient Programs for the Treatment of Psychological Trauma, Handbook of Post-Traumatic Therapy. In: M. B. Williams and J. F. Sommer (eds), *A practical guide to intervention, treatment and research* (pp. 474–491). Westport, CT: Greenwood Publishing.

Burke Harris, N. (2018). *The deepest well: Healing the long-term effects of childhood adversity.* London: Bluebird.

Connected Baby. www.connectedbaby.net.

Gerhardt, S. (2015). *Why love matters,* second edition. Hove: Routledge.

Kolk, van der, B. (2015). *The body keeps the score: Brain, mind, and body in the healing of trauma.* London: Penguin.

KPJR Films. *Resilience: The biology of stress and the science of hope* (documentary). Retrieved from https://kpjrfilms.co/resilience/.

Mate, G. (2019). *When the body says no: Understanding the stress–disease connection.* London: Vermilion.

Mehrit Centre. Self-regulation resources. Retrieved from https://self-reg.ca/.

Merrill, S. (2020). Trauma is 'Written Into Our Bodies' – but educators can help, *Edutopia,* 11 September 2020. Retrieved from https://www.edutopia.org/article/trauma-written-our-bodies-educators-can-help.

Perry, B. and Szalavitz, M. (2017). *The boy who was raised as a dog.* New York, NY: Basic Books.

Porges, S. (2017). *The pocket guide to the polyvagal theory: The transformative power of feeling safe*. New York, NY: W. W. Norton & Company Inc.

Trevarthen, C. (2010). Human nature and early experience. Retrieved from https://vimeo.com/17855175.

World Forum Foundation. Retrieved from https://worldforumfoundation.org/.

Zeedyck, S. Suzanne Zeedyk: The science of human connection. Retrieved from www.suzannezeedyk.com.

POTENTIALITY, MUTUAL ENGAGEMENT AND TRANSFORMATION

ALISTAIR BRYCE-CLEGG

Alistair is an award-winning Early Years author, blogger, product designer and advocate of PLAY. His work has been published in a number of books and magazines and he has worked as an Early Years advisor for various film and television projects.

Alongside support and training for a range of settings and schools, he also works internationally and with Local Authorities across the UK. Most of his time is spent supporting practitioners in their settings or delivering keynotes and training both nationally and internationally. Alistair has an MA in Education and is currently studying for his Doctorate in Early Years. He says that although he is nearing his 30th year in Early Years education, he can remember his first as if it were yesterday.

I am the child of a teacher, which I often think should carry a health warning! My mum was a very talented teacher of what were known in her day as 'top juniors' – what we would refer to now as Year 6. It was listening to her talk at home about school (and we all know how much educators love to talk about work!) and spending time watching her teach when the school I was at had a training day (or what was known as the 'teachers' Christmas shopping day') that I formed lots of my opinions about teaching. I don't just mean the best way to teach addition and subtraction; I am talking about the more subtle ideals that grow to become your fundamental beliefs about what it is to be a teacher, your vision and your values.

When I decided that I wanted to pursue teaching as a career, the seeds of what a 'good' teacher was and what 'effective' practice looked like were already sown. I then went to University to do teacher training and I was again given lots of really clear information about how to teach and what to teach. This added to my concept of best practice. By the time I had been on teaching practice placements and eventually secured my first job, I was really clear about the criteria that would be used to judge whether or not I was successful in my chosen career.

I was also there to witness the birth of the Ofsted inspection as a mechanism for judging effectiveness of schools and even, until fairly recently, grading teachers for meeting various levels of the required standard.

Looking back, it occurs to me that the whole system was based on outcomes and judgement against set criteria. But where did this concept of 'best practice' come from? Was it based in current research or built from myth and tradition?

In my early teaching career I taught as I had been taught to teach. It never occurred to me to question where the philosophy that I was putting into place on a daily basis had come from. I wanted to be the very best I could be and that meant fulfilling the agreed criteria and meeting the standard.

There was also very limited access to any current research in the field. There was no internet, so no social media accounts to follow, no blogs to read and no YouTube to watch. All your information came from books (if you had time to read them), your colleagues and your beloved copies of *Infant Education* magazine – a predecessor of magazines such as *Teach Primary* and *Nursery World*, and a one-stop-shop for all things infant-based!

It wasn't until I embarked on a course of further study that I had the opportunity to re-evaluate my pedagogy and question its source. One of the benefits of further study is that it pushes you to make the time to read things that under normal circumstances you never would have read. Sometimes, especially when it comes to philosophers, this can be difficult and challenging. I have picked up and put down more books than I have finished, but even the most challenging give me something to think about – even if I don't completely understand what they are saying!

I first read Michel Foucault because I had to in order to complete an assignment. I say 'read', but I ordered the book from Amazon and then left it on a pile by my bed until the deadline was looming. Then all I had time to do was dip into the key bits. I would have liked to tell you that I took a weekend and comfortable armchair and immersed myself in the 'Foucaultness of Foucault', but I didn't. The reality is that at the time I was the Headteacher of a large infant school and Early Years unit and had three boys under five years of age at home. If I ever managed to sit in a chair for more than five minutes, you would find me asleep – not immersed in philosophy!

I have revisited Foucault on a number of occasions since then (although I still don't think I understand the Foucaultness of Foucault). But that initial dip into his work alerted me to the concept that he refers to as 'dominant discourses', and that really rang a bell with me. In the education system that we work in we have systems, beliefs and practices we all adhere to. As practitioners, we comply with and facilitate the concept of 'best'. But as a community, we should constantly ask ourselves these questions: 'What is the dominant discourse that runs through our school and education system? Where did it come from and why has its perpetuation been so successful?'

The answer to these questions is multi-layered and complex. A vision for what makes 'best practice' in education has been built up over time, shaped by the politics of the day, sometimes moving towards what was labelled as a more 'child-centred' approach, but fundamentally always coming back to an outcomes-driven system. Our current system of education is built on multiple interpretations and reframing of the work of education pioneers such as Piaget. It has become really clear to me that a lot of the standardised approaches to 'effective' teaching have their roots in a very narrow and singular interpretation of the work of such influential educators, and particularly in Piaget's case, his stages of child development. The popularity of his work and its subsequent application to differing agendas has resulted in it being reduced so that it lacks the complexity that is needed for full understanding, with the result that it is misinterpreted and misapplied. This distorted 'version' of Piaget is then set into longstanding policy and practice.

Piaget worked over several decades, and during that time undoubtedly went through shifts in his own thinking. His work on the identification of children's cognitive development was groundbreaking at the time, and he changed people's perceptions of children by highlighting the cognitive development and capabilities of children. However, breaking Piaget's work down to quantifiable stages of development does not recognise the complexity of the original studies in which Piaget set out to understand the different and multi-layered modes of thinking that children employ during their development. Rather, it just creates a list of concepts that children 'should' have mastered by the time they reach a certain age. This popularised, reduced version of the theory produced an image of the uniform development of children that did not take into account the social and material world around them.

I have found it really good to question what I think I know. It can be an uncomfortable process, but out of that discomfort can come different thinking and effective change. Using current research can be an excellent springboard into directing your thinking. Foucault describes criticism as follows:

A matter of flushing out that thought and trying to change it: to show that things are not as self-evident as one believed, to see that what is accepted as self-evident will no longer be accepted as such ... [A]s soon as one no longer thinks things as one formerly thought them, transformation becomes both very urgent, very difficult, and quite possible. (Foucault, 1988, p. 155)

What is *essential* to enable this process is time. Time to read, time to talk and time to think. It is so easy to push this to the bottom of your 'to do' list when life gets in the way.

In my day-to-day interaction with Early Years practitioners I often find myself encouraging them to reflect on their practice in order to understand it and improve it. Rather than start at the beginning of their education adventure, we start at the end with the 'now' and work backwards to try to establish where their 'now' came from. Why do they do what they do and is it the best and most up-to-date research-based information that we have about effective practice, or do we do it like this because this is how it has always been done?

I know that during the time that I have worked in education my practice has evolved constantly – much faster in recent years than it did at the beginning of my career when I was really focusing on doing what I had been told to do to the best of my ability.

In my current doctoral research I am focusing on the lack of opportunities for enchantment in many Early Years environments. I am defining enchantment as a moment of complete engagement, where the child is taken out of their immediate consciousness by their engagement with the space around them. It is the need for children to have the opportunity to be captivated by a moment, a feeling, an object, a space ... and the transformative possibilities for their development and learning that such an experience could offer.

Research tells us that enchantment seems to inhabit spaces where children have freedom to play and explore – to take control of their own learning and respond to the desires that drive them. You are more likely to find enchantment in a space that has been structured around a Reggio Emilia philosophy than in schools who are responding to a multi-layered political agenda rather than one based on research in education.

It is my sense that many of the adults who work in Early Years education are not aware that they embody the dominant discourse and the 'truths' that result from it. They do not see the power that is moulding their thinking and in turn the power relationship that they participate in with children. The constructions that inhabit learning spaces can never be free of power. They build and reinforce a pedagogical approach to learning that over time comes to 'haunt' every element of even the most complex space. This is why the philosophy of educators like Maria Montessori and Loris Malaguzzi (Reggio Emelia) have come to stand out, labelled as 'different'. These approaches challenge the dominant discourse, and the practitioners who work with them seem to have a significantly different view of themselves as educators and their role as a co-educator alongside the children, the community and the environment. To create more opportunities for enchantment in education, therefore, we need to change the overarching pedagogical approach, deconstructing the dominant discourses so that practitioners can see how they are related to what is going on in their practice. The opportunity to reflect in this way will hopefully also create space to construct an alternative vision for education that is a cooperative and communicative act between child, adult and environment.

I found a huge amount of resonance in the writing of Hillevi Lenz Taguchi. Taguchi is an associate professor in the Department of Education at Stockholm University in Sweden. In lots of her work she challenges our current early education discourses, and through mechanisms like practitioner documentation and reflection she shifts attention from the very binary relationship of the child within the environment to the child as part of the environment, where all material objects have an impact on learning.

I would strongly recommend her book *Going beyond the theory/ practice divide in early childhood education: Introducing an intra-active pedagogy* (2010). In it she details some of her project work, focusing on the importance of artifacts and the environment on children's learning. Taguchi proposes an 'ethics of immanence and potentialities' where the teacher cannot understand the student, the content or the methodology as fixed entities that are separated from everything else.

It is concerned with the inter-connections and intra-actions in-between human and non-human organisms, matter and things, the contents and subjectivities of students that emerge through the learning events. It is concerned with students and teachers in processes of mutual engagement and transformation. (Lenz Taguchi, 2010, p. xvii)

I found the idea of 'potentiality' to be a particularly powerful concept for both children and practitioners. Our current education system is very outcomes driven. As I said previously, educators find themselves in a situation where their effectiveness and worth are judged by the number of children they can enable to meet a standardised requirement. The true and full potential of a child is lost in this very narrow judgement system. Surely a pedagogy for education that is focused on the unique child and how that uniqueness can be cultivated is ultimately desirable?

TOP TIPS

- **Work backwards from your 'what'.** As a practitioner, team and school, spend time clearly articulating what it is that you currently do and then try to trace that 'what' back to its root, looking for references to current and relevant research along the way.
- **Make time to read and think.** It sounds simple enough, but this is a constant aspiration of mine. Sometimes I achieve it; often I don't. But the fact that I am aware of its importance makes it more likely to happen. Some of the settings that I work with have reading groups or staff meetings that are devoted to this sort of activity. Having them scheduled in not only give the process the profile it deserves, it also means they are more likely to happen.
- **Developmentally possible doesn't always mean developmentally appropriate.** Just because children can doesn't mean that they should. Take the time to challenge not only what you do but also how you do it. Think about the routines of your teaching day and how they might impact on children. Remember that the subconscious links that children make to the environment, routines and language that exist within the space are some of the most powerful influences on their learning choices. Compliance is not the same as engagement.

REFERENCES

Foucault, M. (1988). *Politics, Philosophy, Culture: Interviews and Other Writings, 1977–1984.* New York, NY: Routledge, Chapman and Hall, Inc.

Lenz Taguchi, H. (2010). *Going beyond the theory/practice divide in early childhood education: Introducing an intra-active pedagogy.* Abingdon: Routledge.

EARLY CHILDHOOD TEACHERS, EVIDENCE-INFORMED PRACTICE AND TEACHER ACCREDITATION: TALES FROM AUSTRALIA

ALEXANDRA HARPER

Alexandra has worked in education for over 25 years as a teacher and leader across government and independent schooling systems.

Her chapter explores how annotated documentary evidence collected by early childhood teachers as part of the Proficient Teacher accreditation process in New South Wales (NSW) Australia can support evidence-informed practice (EIP) in the Early Childhood Education sector. This is needed because most evidence currently comes from academic research and big data sets. While valuable, these types of evidence do not convey the whole picture, as they miss the nuances that can be captured in teacher-generated evidence. Alexandra's contribution here explores the role teacher accreditation can play in supporting Early Childhood teachers to engage in EIP by using and generating evidence. It also suggests some key lessons for practice.

INTRODUCTION

As an education leader, I have supported many teachers with their teacher accreditation. I have come to see the process: (1) to be an opportunity to collect teacher-generated evidence and (2) to be intellectually engaging, supporting professional collaboration and building teacher capacity and agency. However, this is dependent on a teacher's mindset – notably, whether they see teacher accreditation as an opportunity for professional growth or as primarily a compliance activity. In reality, teacher accreditation is a form of compliance AND an opportunity for professional growth, AND, I would argue, an opportunity for teachers to engage with and generate evidence. This chapter draws on my work in the teacher accreditation space and offers teachers a way of combining current teaching practices with the process of teacher accreditation to engage with and generate evidence.

EVIDENCE-INFORMED PRACTICE AND TEACHER ACCREDITATION IN EARLY CHILDHOOD EDUCATION

Using evidence to inform teaching practice is not new to Early Childhood Education (ECE). Significant figures including Froebel, Isaacs, Montessori, the McMillan sisters and more recently the pedagogues of Reggio Emilia have all drawn on evidence to inform their practice. And not only is evidence-informed practice (EIP) not new, but in Australia it is gaining support, with Early Childhood Teachers (ECTs) being encouraged to engage with and generate evidence. For instance, the CEO of Early Childhood Australia (a national advocacy body) recently stated it is essential that researchers work with ECTs 'to develop evidence-based practices for working with young children'. This is where I believe teacher accreditation can help.

All teachers in New South Wales (NSW) must hold active accreditation in order to teach in a school or service. There are different levels of teacher accreditation – Graduate, Proficient, Highly Accomplished and Lead Teacher. While each level encourages teachers to engage with evidence, the focus of this chapter will be on the process of achieving Proficient Teacher – the mandatory level of accreditation.

Achieving Proficient Teacher recognises that a teacher has met the requirements for full registration into the profession. It is a workplace-based process that supports early career teachers develop their practice against the Standards (NSW Education Standards Authority, 2021).

Teachers complete the process with the support of an accreditation supervisor. There are three components teachers must submit to finalise their accreditation: (1) five to eight pieces of annotated documentary evidence; (2) an Observation Report completed by the teacher's accreditation supervisor after observing their teaching practice; and (3) a Proficient Teacher Accreditation Report written by the teacher's accreditation supervisor. These components cover written and practical aspects of a teacher's practice. The remainder of this chapter will focus on annotated documentary evidence and the role it can play in supporting ECTs to engage in EIP.

AN OVERVIEW OF THE ROLE OF EVIDENCE IN THE PROFICIENT TEACHER ACCREDITATION PROCESS

The Proficient Teacher process supports ECTs to engage in EIP in three ways – by undertaking an evidence-based process; by working with formal research and existing data; and by developing their own evidence.

From the outset, the process of achieving Proficient Teacher is grounded in evidence. This begins with the Standards themselves, which are evidence-based, being built on international and national evidence of 'what teachers should know and be able to do to clarify their role in a knowledge-based profession' (Toledo-Figueroa, Révai and Guerriero, 2017, p. 74). As such, they help 'signal what is expected from teachers and how they can improve at different stages of their professional careers' (Toledo-Figueroa, Révai and Guerriero, 2017, p. 74).

Engaging with research and evidence is also explicitly referred to in the Standards themselves. At Proficient Teacher, this is seen in two Standard Descriptors:

- Structure teaching programs using research and collegial advice about how students learn (Standard Descriptor 1.2.2) and
- Evaluate personal teaching and learning programs using evidence, including feedback from students and student assessment data to inform planning (Standard Descriptor 3.6.2).

(Standard Descriptors are a set of indicators that sit under each of the seven Standards.)

Early in this chapter I mentioned how a teacher's approach and mindset toward teacher accreditation is important. This is because of the level of professional autonomy built into the process. Teachers are not told how they are to engage with the Standards or how to demonstrate meeting the Standards; nor are they expected to provide evidence showing how they meet every Standard Descriptor. Consequently, it is possible for teachers to minimise their engagement with these Standard Descriptors that focus on evidence. I would argue that this is a missed opportunity.

Lastly, the Proficient Teacher process invites teachers to generate evidence via the mandate to collect and annotate evidence that is 'naturally harvested' from their daily work (Toledo-Figueroa, Révai and Guerriero, 2017). When annotating evidence, a teacher is expected to explain how two to four self-nominated Standard Descriptors are demonstrated in their evidence. This requires ECTs to critically reflect on their practice. This may be done independently and/or in collaboration with colleagues. What this may look like is considered in the next section.

THE ROLE OF CRITICAL REFLECTION IN SUPPORTING EIP

'It changed my teaching in that I now think more critically about the learning that is occurring.' (Teacher)

The importance of critical reflection and its impact on teaching practice cannot be overstated. Recently, a project found that planned critical reflection and practices of critical reflection were a determining factor in Early Childhood services meeting the NQS for Educational Program and Practice. Furthermore, the study found that the level of critical reflection played a role in services achieving either a 'meeting' or 'exceeding' NQS assessment rating (Harrison, et al., 2019). Interestingly, this project also found that the type of critical reflection is important, as those services rated as exceeding NQS reflected on teaching practices and the children's behaviour. It is worth noting here that critical reflection as outlined by the NQS is an expectation of services and not teachers.

I would argue that engaging in critical reflection, while not a requirement by NESA (New South Wales Education Standards Authority), helps teachers write effective annotations that are required to accompany documentary evidence submitted as part of the Proficient Teacher accreditation process.

Some questions that the teachers I have worked with have found useful to support critical reflection include:

- How do I see my teaching practice through the lens of the Standards?
- Which Standard Descriptors are best demonstrated in this evidence of my teaching practice?
- Which Standard Descriptors can I not provide evidence for and how can I develop these aspects of my teaching practice?

Asking questions like these helps teachers critically examine evidence collected from their teaching to inform their practice. In my experience most teachers are able to do this, excepting those teachers who are struggling with their practice. In these cases, the Proficient Teacher accreditation process provides a useful framework for them to gently interrogate their practice with the support of a supervisor. As such, annotating documentary evidence provides a unique opportunity for teachers to use evidence derived from their practice for self-improvement while meeting regulatory requirements. For a profession that is time poor, this is a welcomed prospect.

Additionally, as previously argued, teacher accreditation provides a way for ECTs to introduce a previously missing piece of EIP – teacher-generated evidence. In collecting and annotating their practice, ECTs are making teaching visible. This provides an opportunity to complement exisiting formal academic research and big data sets with teacher-generated evidence. An additional benefit is the 'unearthing' of contextualised data that provides information about the kinds of teaching practices that do or do not work for specific children and/ or specific contexts. This information would be welcomed given the diversity of contexts across NSW. Excitingly for teachers, they do not have to create new documents, but rather consider new ways of discussing their practice through the lens of the service AND the child AND their teaching practice. The Proficient Teacher process helps with the latter.

THE ROLE OF PROFESSIONAL COLLABORATION IN SUPPORTING EIP

'It was a rewarding experience in that we had a collaboration meeting with other teachers that were starting their accreditation process as well.' (Teacher)

Teacher accreditation also provides an opportunity for ECTs to engage with evidence through collaboration and professional discussions. This is achieved by bringing existing research and data into discussions through the aforementioned Standard Descriptors and colleagues coming together to critically reflect on self-generated evidence.

Teacher accreditation facilitates this in two ways. Firstly, the Standards promote professional discussions as seen in Standard Descriptor 6.3.2: 'contribute to collegial discussions and apply constructive feedback from colleagues to improve professional knowledge and practice' (NSW Education Standards Authority, 2014). Secondly, the process supports professional collaboration between a teacher and their supervisor and between colleagues.

When working as a supervisor, I found conversations critical. It was through conversation that I built positive professional relationships. I found the Standards played an important role in ensuring the conversations were targeted and productive. They did this by blending technical knowledge with exploration and a discussion of research. Some of the richest conversations occurred when teachers used the Standards to identify areas of strength and areas of growth. Often these discussions led to affirmation of current practice. Other times they helped identify opportunities to try something new, with the teacher undertaking an action research project. Teacher accreditation has created the space and given permission to engage in EIP. As one teacher remarked, 'We never get time to have these discussions. Accreditation gives us this opportunity.'

Professional collaboration can extend beyond the supervisor–teacher relationship to teacher networks. Some of the most rewarding experiences I have enjoyed in this space are where I have brought teachers working towards Proficient Teacher together to discuss and unpack the Standards. The discussions were rich, powerful and focused, and fostered 'a collegial culture of sharing' (Gu, 2017). I recall a lengthy discussion relating to Standard Descriptor 5.1.2 – 'develop, select and use informal and formal, diagnostic, formative and summative assessment strategies to assess student learning' – and what this looks like in the Early Childhood context. The teachers left the meeting with a common goal – to collect evidence of the assessment practices in their services and to explore what they could find in research. At the next meeting, they shared the evidence and research articles they had collected. The resultant discussion revealed the complex, sophisticated and evidence-informed ways ECTs assess children's learning. It helped make teaching visible. Furthermore, grounding the conversation in the common language of the Standards allowed the ECTs to transcend their different contexts, and in doing so minimise the previously cited issues associated with the fragmentation of the ECE sector.

While not specific to EIP, another important benefit of professional collaboration is that it can promote feelings of professional joy and support, especially during times of reform when teachers are experiencing stress and frustration (Datnow, 2018). Teachers I have worked with have shared these sentiments and said that working with others reduced feelings of isolation and helped keep them on track. One teacher reported that 'it makes the process more than just ticking a box'.

However, professional collaboration is not without its challenges. For instance, some ECTs working in remote locations find it hard to physically connect with their colleagues. Saying this, one benefit of the changes necessitated during the COVID-19 pandemic has been that they have shown us how we can use technology to connect. However, this brings with it another question – how, when isolated and working within a fragmented sector, do you find teachers to connect with? This also does not address another barrier – ECTs who find themselves working in a service that does not value cross-service collaboration and actively works against the sharing of intellectual capital.

So, what does all this mean? What are the key takeaways for ECTs?

TOP TIPS

(Please note the following suggestions are by no means exhaustive and are presented to promote further discussion and exploration.)

- **Create the win–win.**
  Embrace 'YES … AND'. Compliance and regulation can be an opportunity for professional growth and to engage with research. It doesn't have to be either/or. This requires a shift in thinking and adopting a new mindset. Yes, I have to 'do' teacher accreditation AND I am going to engage in evidence-informed professional growth. Practice and policy can co-exist. All that is needed is a willingness to think differently.
- **Embrace the opportunity to connect with others.**
  I think I have covered this extensively in the previous section, but it is worth mentioning again. Teacher accreditation can help promote connection by inviting teachers to come together to share and reflect on their teaching practice as they collect and annotate their evidence.
- **Get creative. Embrace intellectual challenge.**
  While the accreditation process is task specific, there is room to make it so much more than a compliance exercise. It can be creative. Teacher accreditation gives teachers the opportunity to take risks, innovate and explore what the Standards look like in their unique contexts.

- **Use your annotated documentary evidence to make your teaching visible in ECE and beyond.**
Annotated documentary evidence makes the teaching of ECE visible. Sharing this work would benefit all ECTs. Furthermore, given that the Standards are common to all phases of education, the annotated documentary evidence could be shared with other phases. I believe primary and secondary teachers could learn a great deal from their Early Childhood colleagues, specifically in the areas of authentic learning, critical and creative thinking and how to document teaching practice.

REFERENCES

Datnow, A. (2018). Time for change? The emotions of teacher collaboration and reform, *Journal of Professional Capital and Community* 3(2), 157–172. doi:10.1108/JPCC-12-2017-0028.

Early Childhood Australia (15 June 2020). Media release: National evidence institute can help ensure a great start to every child's education.

Gu, Q. (2017). Relationships matter: Fostering and sustaining resilient teachers, *Professional Development Today* 19(2), 18–26.

Harrison, L. J., Hadley, F., Irvine, S., Davis, B., Barblett, L., Hatzigianni, M., Mulhearn, G., Waniganayake, M. and Li, P. (November 2019). Quality Improvement Research Project. Commissioned by the Australian Children's Education and Care Quality Authority (ACECQA). Retrieved from https://www.acecqa.gov.au/sites/default/files/2020-05/quality-improvement-research-project-2019.PDF.

NSW Education Standards Authority (2014). Australian Professional Standards for Teachers. Sydney: NSW Education Standards Authority. Retrieved from https://educationstandards.nsw.edu.au/wps/wcm/connect/8658b2fa-62d3-40ca-a8d9-02309a2c67a1/australian-professional-standards-teachers.pdf?MOD=AJPERES&CVID=.

NSW Education Standards Authority (2021). Teacher accreditation. Apply for Proficient Teacher Accreditation. Retrieved from https://educationstandards.nsw.edu.au/wps/portal/nesa/teacher-accreditation/apply/proficient-teacher.

Toledo-Figueroa, D., Révai, N. and Guerriero, S. (2017). Teacher professionalism and knowledge in qualifications frameworks and professional standards. In S. Guerriero (ed.), *Pedagogical knowledge and the changing nature of the teaching profession* (pp. 73–95). Paris: OECD Publishing. doi:http://dx.doi.org/10.1787/9789264270695-en.

CHILDREN'S AGENCY AND THE CURRICULUM

DOMINIC WYSE

Dominic Wyse is Professor of Early Childhood and Primary Education at University College London (UCL) Institute of Education (IOE). He is President of the British Educational Research Association (BERA) and Founding Director of the Helen Hamlyn Centre for Pedagogy (0–11). Dominic is a Fellow of the Academy of Social Sciences (FAcSS) and a Fellow of the Royal Society for the Encouragement of Arts, Manufactures and Commerce (RSA).

The main focus of Dominic's research is curriculum and pedagogy. His research has contributed to an understanding of the pedagogy of writing, reading, literacy and creativity across the life course (e.g. *How writing works: From the invention of the alphabet to the rise of social media* (Cambridge University Press) and *The good writing guide for education students*, 4th edition (Sage)). Dominic has extensive experience of working at the interface of research, policy and practice (e.g. see the BERA Close-to-practice research project (https://www.bera.ac.uk/project/close-to-practice-research-project) or Wyse and Torgerson (2017), Experimental trials and 'what works?' in education: The case of grammar for writing published in the *British Educational Research Journal*). One of his current research projects is the Grammar and Writing project (funded by the Nuffield Foundation). Bestselling books for students, teachers and educators include *Teaching English, language and literacy*, 4th edition (Routledge) (including a special edition for students in South Africa). From 2012 to 2018 Dominic was one of the editors of *The Curriculum Journal (BERA)*.

INTRODUCTION

Being 'research-informed' means having an understanding of the ways in which research can help people to make decisions about improvements in life. Being research-informed does not just affect those working in education; it is an issue for the whole of society. For example, take the COVID-19 context. Researchers provide evidence about COVID-19. The government, and society in general, have to interpret the guidance from scientists. People then have to make decisions about how to follow the government advice. Those people who attend carefully to the research to inform their behaviour are research-informed; those who ignore the research are not. Naturally, there are different levels of being research-informed, ranging from a layperson who occasionally follows summaries of research in the mainstream media to someone who is a senior researcher doing research.

It is very rare for research to provide a final, definitive answer about questions that affect society, including for research in the natural sciences. Take smoking as an example. In the 1950s the first experimental trials showed a causal effect between smoking cigarettes and the chances of people getting lung cancer. A causal relationship is one where we can say confidently, on the basis of valid and reliable research, that X causes Y. Causal effects are nearly always very demanding to prove, particularly in areas of human life that are social in character rather than physiological. Yet even with the example of the causal effect of smoking, it took until the 2000s for the first bans on smoking in public places to be introduced. The 50-year delay was caused by a range of factors, not least organisations and people who actively campaigned to dispute the causal findings made by scientists (Oreskes and Conway, 2011). And, of course, despite the science, people continue to smoke. So one of the most important elements about being research-informed is to realise that it requires the *interpretation* of research followed by *choices* and decisions about how to respond. A basic element of being research-informed is to understand that the issues are nearly always complex and almost never rest on single research studies.

This book is not, of course, about pandemics or smoking; it is about education and research. My chosen education focus in this chapter is children's agency and the curriculum, because, in my view and based on my expertise, these are particularly important areas of knowledge for teachers, and curriculum raises suitably complex questions about the place of research in relation to practice and policy.

BEGINNING TO UNDERSTAND CURRICULUM STUDY

Most teachers regard the curriculum as an important topic because it reflects an essential part of what children learn every day and is central to teachers' and other educators' practice. An evidence-informed understanding of curriculum reveals it as a multi-faceted topic that is influenced by a range of different kinds of questions. Here is a small selection:

- To what extent should an Early Years curriculum be play-based?
- Is a child-centred curriculum more effective than a teacher-directed curriculum?
- To what extent are breadth and balance important in a curriculum?
- Should knowledge drive national curriculum models?
- Should a curriculum be organised as subjects or as broader areas of learning?
- What is the most effective way to teach particular subjects in the curriculum?
- Are 'core' subjects more important than 'foundation' subjects?

It is appropriate that I have begun this exploration of research-informed practice with questions, because questions are where all research starts. Research is driven by curiosity about an aspect of human experience that the researcher or researchers are interested in. If the research is to be pursued rigorously, then clear research questions are written down in order to focus the research and to aid in the selection of the methods of research that will in the end answer the questions effectively.

One of the key topics for the study of curriculum is the extent to which the curriculum should be determined by teachers, schools and national curriculum policy as opposed to being informed by pupils' perspectives and life contexts. We might use this as an overarching research question:

To what extent should children's agency by part of curriculum planning and pedagogy in Early Years and Primary School settings?

Perhaps the most important point to make at the outset is that this question is very broad, and it is complex to research. In terms of a research project, it would need breaking down into sub-questions in order to develop a workable research design. However, the question does reflect a topic that is of interest to teachers, policymakers and researchers. It is also clearly related to the topic of child-centred versus teacher-directed curriculum that I included in the list of questions above – a topic that has a very long history.

Any good research project begins with the researchers' thorough and precise knowledge of previously published research. This is often developed through a 'literature review'. The literature review reflects researchers' knowledge about the field of study that can sometimes account for trends of research over decades. This historical perspective is rather important for curriculum study, because so-called solutions to curriculum questions need to take account of practices and policies that have been tried in the past and have not worked sufficiently to help children's learning. I re-emphasise here that a good review of previously published research is cautious about singling out individual research studies, because all research has limitations in its methods, and besides, any published paper or book is only one research team's view of the topic.

A research method that has grown in popularity over the last two decades is called 'systematic review'. This can be seen as a rigorous way of reviewing the literature in a given field. The review is 'systematic' because specific methods are used to ensure that the selection of published research studies is not just based on researchers' preferences, but follows criteria for inclusion and exclusion of studies, linked carefully to a set of research questions that inform the systematic review. The use of inclusion and exclusion criteria is important, because too often people, including politicians, 'cherry-pick' one study to back up their ideology rather than take a balanced view of the range of studies addressing a particular research topic (a seminal paper in relation to the teaching of reading unpicks a case like this: Wyse and Goswami, 2008). However, even single systematic reviews are not the last word – in some popular research areas there are reviews of multiple systematic reviews! Someone who is research-informed has awareness of the value of multiple research studies. They are less likely to propose simplistic solutions to practical problems backed up by single studies with dubious credibility. Dubious studies can be put in their proper place and, if necessary, rejected as an influence on practice.

As far as curriculum research is concerned, to my knowledge there have not been sufficient numbers of quantitative studies comparing the effectiveness of whole curriculum approaches to be collected together in a systematic review and meta-analysis (statistical comparison that is part of some systematic reviews of studies that report Effect Sizes). There are, however, other robust sources that can help our thinking about curriculum, some of which I describe later in this chapter.

CHALLENGES TO BEING RESEARCH-INFORMED

Apart from levels of understanding of how research works, another challenge to becoming research-informed is simply the amount of research in the world! For professional people whose work demands large amounts of time devoted to their core job, it is very challenging to read lots of research papers, chapters and books. However, this is where Master's degrees and Doctorates are so important. In universities, Master's degrees and then doctorates are seen as researchers' early research training, and the beginning of the journey is getting to grips with a particular field of research – in effect becoming more research-informed. It all begins with reviewing literature. And a good doctorate is not just a preparation for future research; it can in the right circumstances result in a paper or book being published by the student. What follows is a brief example of a doctoral study that is relevant to child-centred education, Early Years and the issue of being research-informed.

One of my doctoral student's research focused on the use of digital technology in nursery education. Although her literature review synthesised many studies from around the world, her preferred research method was to prioritise depth over breadth, so she focused in depth in her work on one nursery teacher. The research method was Education Design Research (EDR). Often EDR features an intervention designed in collaboration with practitioners. The intervention is then subject to evaluation through research, and reflections about the process and about the intervention itself lead to changes in practice. For me, the most striking outcome of the research was to learn how an experienced Early Years teacher with a commitment to child-centred education, but also a strong scepticism about use of digital technology in her classroom, was enabled to challenge her long-held beliefs and develop a new classroom approach that enabled her to plan for using digital technologies in a child-centred way (you can read about the research in the peer-reviewed research paper by Vidal-Hall, Flewitt and Wyse, 2020).

In view of the challenges of time to read research papers and books, it has long been recognised that professional people require straightforward access to robust summaries of research that are relevant to their questions. Over more than 30 years, there have been many attempts to achieve this. Here is a very brief selection of things that are available now or have been tried in the past:

- Twitter. Massive worldwide reach, and can raise awareness of research. Tends to result in one-sided views of topics because of the way people follow people they like rather than people who might offer an alternative perspective. Brevity of messages leads to multiple interpretations and confusions.
- *Nursery World*. Popular magazine clearly focused on issues for Early Years workers. Like most media outlets, tends to favour single researchers and single projects, and usually only if considered topical.
- Google/Google Scholar. Perhaps the way most people start their search these days. Requires considerable knowledge, and time, to

identify *robust* research that is relevant to a particular research question. There are bespoke tools accessible through universities, such as the British Education Index (BEI), which only include research publications rather than everything in the world!

- Education Endowment Foundation. Useful 'toolkits' aimed at professionals. Like most funders, has an emphasis on the projects they have funded (via government funding). Restricted to research that uses experimental research design methods, which are very good for comparison of effectiveness of tightly focused interventions but not as good for many other research questions.
- British Educational Research Association. Third largest education research organisation in the world. Includes Special Interest Group (SIG) on Early Years (https://www.bera.ac.uk/community/early-childhood-education-and-care). BERA is more focused on supporting members than summarising particular areas of research, although this is a growth area, including the Presidential Round Tables; BERA Blog; and Research Intelligence.
- Chartered College of Teaching (CCT). Relatively new and growing in importance. *Impact* journal is a good example that includes overviews of research areas (see example relevant to children's agency: Norman, Manyukhina and Wyse, 2020). Also the CCT's Education Exchange (e.g. Wyse & Manyukhina, 2020).
- The Teaching and Learning Research Project (TLRP) was funded by the Higher Education Funding Council/Economic and Social Research Council. Largest set of projects in the UK all focusing on aspects of education. Diverse projects and not many devoted to Early Years education. Longer history to TLRP than some other sources, but TLRP principles still relevant (e.g. new book, for which I am lead editor, *Reflective Teaching in Primary Schools*, being developed for 2021 will continue to reflect the TLRP principles).
- The Teacher Training Resource Bank (archived here https://webarchive.nationalarchives.gov.uk/20101021152907/http://www.ttrb.ac.uk/#) – closed many years ago, and somewhat eclectic, but

the TTRB selected outputs relevant to teacher training and then had them peer-reviewed and short summary reports presented. Indicative of the problem of not sustaining an access source because of cuts in government funding.

CURRICULUM AND CHILDREN'S AGENCY – A RESEARCH STUDY

The study described in this section was research-informed, and linked research, policy and practice in many different ways. Most important of all was the funder's desire to ensure that the national curriculum development in Ireland was evidence informed, built over a sustained period, and a partnership between all stakeholders. My colleague Yana Manyukhina and I were commissioned by Ireland's Curriculum Agency (the National Council for Curriculum and Assessment (NCCA)) to carry out a study of knowledge in the curriculum (the peer-reviewed research paper reporting the findings of the research is Manyukhina and Wyse, 2020. See also the other references in this chapter to other formats that have been used to disseminate the work). We were asked to arrive at a recommended way of defining knowledge in what was to be the new primary curriculum in Ireland. The research included a comparison of national curriculum texts in four jurisdictions worldwide.

The invitation to carry out the work in the first place was because of my research expertise in Early Years and Primary curriculum. This is another example of being research-informed to a professorial level. My previous research had included being part of a study of creativity in what were the 27 countries of the EU (Wyse and Ferrari, 2014), and a role in the expert review of curriculum and assessment for the Cambridge Primary Review (Wyse & Torrance, 2009). In addition, I was one of the editors of the BERA *Curriculum Journal* for six years and the lead editor for the two-volume *SAGE Handbook of Curriculum, Pedagogy and Assessment* (Wyse, Hayward and Pandya, 2015). All of those projects contributed to my own level of being research active, but also made different kinds of contributions to the study of curriculum.

Like any research project, there was a range of findings from the Ireland national curriculum project that we did, but in order to end this chapter I will focus on just one finding. The review of the national curriculum texts of four countries/regions that were high performing in international comparative pupil tests showed just how different England's national curriculum was when compared to the three other countries. Whereas in Hong Kong the national curriculum strongly emphasises children's agency, in England the emphasis is on knowledge. The reason that England's national curriculum is heavily knowledge-based is because Michael Gove, who was Secretary of State for Education, did not take sufficient account of the views of the expert panel, preferring instead to allow political ideology to influence the curriculum (for evidence of this position see James, 2012). Being research-informed also means that I have to acknowledge that our research project was an analysis of national curriculum texts and did not involve any empirical work in Early Years or Primary School settings in the different countries (because of the specifications of the commission), so it has limitations.

What this story of children's agency and the curriculum shows us is that although research evidence can tell us very important things about curriculum (e.g. the most effective ways to teach literacy), there are also important ethical and moral dimensions to the study, practice and policy of curriculum development. However, my view, based on a range of multi-disciplinary evidence, is that greater emphasis on children's agency is likely to improve their education and hence life chances.

TOP TIPS

- Beware of a too heavy focus on the findings of one research study. Remember that it usually takes many research studies over many years to provide strong evidence to support a particular education decision.
- Seek out opportunities to collaborate with researchers on research projects.
- Consider doing a Master's degree and/or Doctorate to help your ambition to be research-informed.

REFERENCES

James, M. (2012). Background to Michael Gove's response to the Report of the Expert Panel for the National Curriculum Review in England, *BERA News*. Retrieved from https://www.bera.ac.uk/bera-in-the-news/background-to-michael-goves-response-to-the-report-of-the-expert-panel-for-the-national-curriculum-review-in-england.

Manyukhina, Y. and Wyse, D. (2019). Learner agency and the curriculum: A critical realist perspective, *The Curriculum Journal* 30(3), 223–243. DOI:10.1 080/09585176.2019.1599973.

Norman, G., Manyukhina, Y. and Wyse, D. (forthcoming). A difficult partnership? Pupil agency and the National Curriculum, *Impact: Journal of the Chartered College of Teaching*.

Oreskes, N. and Conway, E. (2011). *The Merchants of Doubt*. London: Bloomsbury.

Vidal-Hall, C., Flewitt, R. and Wyse, D. (2020). Early childhood practitioner beliefs about digital media: Integrating technology into a child-centred classroom environment, *European Early Childhood Education Research Journal*. DOI: 10.1080/1350293X.2020.1735727.

Wyse, D. (2017). *How Writing Works: From the invention of the alphabet to the rise of social media*. Cambridge: Cambridge University Press.

Wyse, D. and Cowan, K. (2012). *The good writing guide for education students* (Sage Study Skills Series), 4th edition. London: Sage Publications Ltd.

Wyse, D. and Ferrari, A. (2014). Creativity and education: Comparing the national curricula of the states of the European Union with the United Kingdom, *British Educational Research Journal*, 41(1), 30–47.

Wyse, D. and Goswami, U. (2008). Synthetic phonics and the teaching of reading, *British Educational Research Journal* 34(6), 691–710.

Wyse, D., Hayward, L. and Pandya, J. (eds.) (2015). *The SAGE handbook of curriculum, pedagogy and assessment*. London: SAGE.

Wyse, D., Jones, R., Bradford, H. and Wolpert, M. A. (2018). *Teaching English, language and literacy*. Abgingdon: Routledge.

Wyse, D. and Manyukhina, Y. (2020). Children's agency and the curriculum. The Education Exchange from the Chartered College of Teachers. Retrieved from https://theeducation.exchange/childrens-agency-and-the-curriculum/.

Wyse, D. and Torgerson, C. (2017). Experimental trials and 'what works?' in education: The case of grammar for writing, *British Educational Research Journal* 43(6), 1019–1047.

Wyse, D. and Torrance, H. (2009). The development and consequences of national curriculum assessment for primary education in England, *Educational Research* 51(2), 213–228.

IT STARTED WITH DOUGH DISCO

SHONETTE BASON-WOOD

Shonette Bason-Wood qualified as a Primary School teacher in 1993, which she says makes her an old teacher! She has taught various age ranges in many different locations, including Cyprus, but her passion is the Early Years child. Her great enthusiasm for Early Years started with a Reception class that was extremely challenging with their behaviour, which meant she had to adapt her traditional teaching style for a much more outdoor- and movement-based approach. The reason she switched teaching style is because she is the mother of four children who are a year apart. At one stage, she had four children under the age of four, which is when she developed a lot of practical skills for how to manage very young children whilst maintaining her sanity. The main parent strategy she used was physical development. Each day, with a strict routine in place, she included a large amount of daily exercise, mainly walking or – in the winter months (UK winters) – in soft play for hours.

On my first meeting with the class that changed everything, I walked into the temporary accommodation where they were attending nursery and realised very quickly that they were not only predominantly boys, but also very high energy! The room felt like a pressure cooker about to explode, and the boys were role playing police officers and hitting each other with pretend truncheons – not quite an image of the police one wants to develop!! I knew from my experience with my own four children that exercise to expend that energy was going to be a key factor in my planning for these children.

My initial approach was probably instinctive, coming from my own experience as a child and with my own children; it was that as an integral part of development children needed to be outside walking, exploring and having adventures. I honestly didn't know why I just knew it worked.

I decided that an outdoor curriculum was imperative, and I spent the summer planning and organising this in our small outside area. I set up clear routines and structures with exciting activities. The impact was very quick, and the children became more ready to learn. This then led me to examine how I was going to motivate this lively but intelligent class to learn, now that I had their behaviour under control. I knew a traditional type of curriculum would not cut it with these children and that I needed to find/design a curriculum that would not only engage the children, but develop their learning too.

I started to research the importance of movement in learning, came across Neuro-Linguistic Programming and attended a conference on this. I was absolutely fascinated by what I learnt, especially that when a young child learns the parts of the body, their fingers are the last part the brain recognises. This had a huge impact on me, because children are often taught to write through copying and perhaps guided by adults holding the pencil with them! I went on to read mainly Sally Goddard Blythe's work on neuro movement and education. We had a Neuro Developmental Practitioner come into school to present a session with staff and work with the children across the school.

As I watched closely the work of the Neuro Developmental Practitioner with Key Stage 2, I observed that they regularly did an exercise before writing called tapping. It works the fine muscle because fine muscle, like gross muscle, needs consistent exercise once developed. The tapping on an object also gave the brain excellent fine muscle control. My brain started to work overtime as I realised that the developing brain takes six human years to learn to control the body and that the fingers, as I referred to already, are the last thing it learns to control. My movement-based approach meant minimal furniture within my classroom to maximise movement indoors and out. I thought, *all children love dough and all children love music, so why not combine the two? Plus, music is so motivational, especially disco music.* It was from this I developed Dough Disco, a fine muscle exercise.

The results were quite amazing. Based on the work of Jack A. Nagleiri, at the start of a six-week trial I asked the children to draw a person totally unaided. Six weeks later, I asked them to draw a person again, and every child had made progress, including the children with special educational needs. With this evidence, I was able to win over the Senior Leadership Team to continue with the work. With the success of Dough Disco accelerating fine muscle control, I then investigated more ways to accelerate early development, simply adding movement to traditional teaching styles.

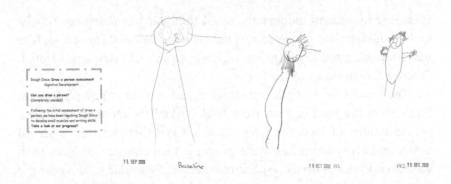

My work became quite well known in the educational field and I was invited to the University of Oxford to discuss movement and the brain with Baroness Susan Greenfield. She then invited me to the House of Lords to take part in a debate on the importance of neuroscience within the development of young children. My work was discussed by the working party, and her Oxford University neuroscience team agreed that Dough Disco was an outstanding way to develop early fine muscle control.

I learnt, through my research into neuroscience, that it was important in the development of a young child to activate both sides of the brain, so I decided to explore this further and look at how I could develop children's actual writing skills without laborious copying and worksheets. This is how I came to develop Squiggle Whilst you Wiggle, a sequenced writing programme using movement. From research, I discovered that S is the hardest letter for a child to form, yet it is one of the letters/sounds we had previously taught first. Squiggle Whilst you Wiggle teaches writing letters in a sequential way based on body movement and body coordination; again, this approach accelerates children's ability to write. From here, I went on to develop further programmes in writing and reading, all very different from the time-honoured ways of teaching, but with great results. A revolution!!

When I first started out with this movement-based approach to learning, I met with a lot of scepticism, not only from my own team but within school. Teachers who were used to the traditional tables and chairs style of teaching find the movement-based approach challenging,

I believe, because they haven't taken into account the fact that childhood has changed. I was born 1972. My childhood was mainly outdoors and I had a lot more freedom than many children have nowadays. As I implemented a movement-based approach with passion, purpose and energy, my team quickly came on board. They themselves saw the transformational results with the children and also the fun that everyone was having. When I explained the neurological science behind the development they were seeing in the children, they realised that the increase in progress had firm science behind the practice and therefore had to be taken seriously. The rest of the school was a little harder. I did a presentation to Governors, two of whom had children in my class, and they were highly supportive of my continuing the approach and going out to other schools. I also did a presentation to other staff where the commonly held belief was that all we did in Early Years was 'play'. I also invited them to come and observe, which some took advantage of. Those who came were surprised not only at how hard all the staff worked, but at how the children from the age of three were engaged with learning (even reading and writing).

There have been many theories over the years on how children learn, but I strongly believe that the research on the influence of neuroscience in a child's development is the most relevant today. As we well know, this is a digitised world, and in recent research it was found that 49 per cent of 3- to 4-year-olds have access to mobile devices and go online (Ofcom, 2019). Our children are, as Sue Palmer (2015) calls it, in a 'toxic childhood', and movement and playing outdoors, etc. are no longer prevalent activities for children. It is therefore vitally important for educators to ensure that we address this gap by offering children learning through an active lifestyle. Many of our children are developmentally delayed as a result of the electronic world, and our role is not to berate over this but to address it. At the same time, I often smile at the IT side of the curriculum where children are taught to use a mouse, when they can probably outshine us with digital devices even at the age of three!

Whilst I travelled around the country and the world, one thing that became very apparent to me is that some people were not happy in their role working with children – 'the lemon suckers', as I call them. I decided that happiness should be an important component in education and designed the Whole School Happiness Approach, which is a five-week programme for Early Years and Primary Schools aimed at supporting the wellbeing of both adults and children and of the wider community. Prior to writing the programme, I researched the science of happiness and found that it *is* actually a science!! Being happy releases serotonin in the brain, which contributes to wellbeing. This research is now the basis to my keynote speeches and of a recently published book.

My trainings around the country and the world are often sell-outs, and we now run accredited courses for teachers to become skilled in teaching the Spread the Happiness way. All this from one simple fine muscle exercise!!

TOP TIPS

So here are my three main tips on starting the revolution in Early Years:

• If you want to start movement-based learning within your own setting, then I suggest you gather as much evidence as you can and put together a presentation on the importance of movement-based learning in order to present to the relevant people and to prepare for Ofsted and for parents/carers. Start small with Dough Disco initially so as not to overwhelm them.

   Knowledge is a persuasive power, and within society everyone believes they know how to teach because everyone went to school, but it is often based on the way they were taught!

   So arm yourself with knowledge through published works and research, listen to podcasts, watch TED Talks and YouTube. Search engines are amazing tools and instantly available to support your learning. There is also a wealth of online courses. But be selective. Look at courses that are based on research and have validity. You could even buy good old-fashioned books that you can refer to time and time again!

Sometimes we become enmeshed in the everyday job in the classroom and time becomes limited. It is vitally important to continue to learn and grow in order to stay ahead of the game and be the best educator you can be, so set aside some time each week specifically allocated to your own professional development.

- Be brave. If you truly believe in any new initiatives and approaches, then put your case forward to the powers that be in a reasoned and well-presented way with evidence that it works. If they don't take it on board, perhaps you could ask for a six-week trial period to demonstrate the impact – even link it to your appraisal if you dare!! If this doesn't work, it is time to move to a new and more forward-thinking setting!!
- I firmly believe that to be the best educator you can be it is important to look after your own happiness first in order to have an impact on your colleagues and the children. Do not become too intense and obsessive about wanting to introduce new approaches. Look at the awe and wonder in the children and absorb that for yourself. Keep the fun and never forget the reason you wanted to become an educator in the first place – to make a difference in young children's lives!

REFERENCES

Goddard Blythe, S. (2005). *The well balanced child: Movement and early learning.* Stroud: Hawthorn Press.

Goddard Blythe, S. (2009). *Attention balance and coordination – the A.B.C. of learning success.* Chichester: Wiley.

Ofcom (2019). Children and Parents: media use and attitudes report. Retrieved from https://www.ofcom.org.uk/__data/assets/pdf_file/0023/190616/children-media-use-attitudes-2019-report.pdf.

Palmer, S. (2015). *Toxic childhood: How the modern world is damaging our children and what we can do about it.* London: Orion.

RESEARCH INTO PRACTICE – OUTDOORS

JULIE MOUNTAIN

A landscape designer by profession, Julie has spent 25 years working with schools and Early Years settings in the UK and beyond, helping them focus on creating, resourcing and managing high-quality outdoor spaces and places.

In addition to her Early Years outdoors design projects, Julie provides immersive Continuing Professional Development (CPD) programmes, writes for magazines and journals and runs an outdoors-all-day holiday club.

Learning and playing outdoors is crucial for children's health and wellbeing and makes significant contributions to learning outcomes.

This is true for learners of all ages, but is particularly apposite for our youngest learners, for whom the whole world – indoors and out – is a magical place, ripe for exploration. Over a career spanning almost 30 years, I've visited hundreds of schools and settings, absorbed countless books, papers, blogs and articles, and fallen over in the mud more times than I care to remember. My faith in the importance of robust research-informed outdoor practice only increases.

There are two fundamental strands to my work: helping schools and settings remodel their outdoor spaces and providing Continuing Professional Development (CPD) that will ensure outdoor spaces are used to their maximum potential, regardless of size, shape, character or facilities. These two elements are absolutely interdependent, and my pedagogical approach to learning and playing outdoors has been shaped by key research discoveries along the way.

As I write, with the final days of 2020 in sight, I note that it took a pandemic to convince mainstream education that outdoors should be an essential part of every child's day, despite high-quality, robust academic research and the professional experiences of thousands of educators demonstrating precisely this for well over one hundred years. It suggests that whilst the content of the message – outdoors is a great place for learning, play and health outcomes – is strong, its delivery has not yet been strong enough to overcome barriers to its wholesale adoption by schools and settings.

Schools and settings present common 'barriers' to taking learning outdoors or to spending more time outdoors. These include (but are not limited to): practitioners' own confidence; time in a crowded day; lack of understanding of the value of outdoors; belief that 'stuff' is needed to make outdoors work properly; and risk aversion. I've found that a combination of research-informed exemplars and shared action research is an effective way of helping practitioners overcome this.

As such, my provision of CPD has changed over the years. When I first began applying my landscape design skills to the challenge of school grounds and nursery gardens, most CPD for educators took place on a 'Baker Day' or a twilight session – or perhaps squeezed into a couple of staff meetings. ('Baker Days' were in-service training days introduced by then Education Secretary Kenneth Baker in 1988. They are now more commonly known as Inset days.) Technological advances, married with the sector's growing understanding of what the C in CPD actually stands for, means CPD providers are now able to engage with their adult learners over longer periods, and in a myriad of immersive ways. Now, it's unusual to be asked to provide a 'pit-stop' one-day training event, and evidence shows that connecting with interactive, longer-term learning helps embed that learning more effectively. As educators, we know that children need agency over their learning and that complex problems require time and effort to master. The same is true of adults (Peters, 2004).

CASE STUDY: OUTDOORS & ACTIVE, NEWHAM, LONDON

To illustrate how this works in practice, let me share a programme I was invited to lead in the London Borough of Newham and on behalf of Early Education. The programme, Outdoors & Active, conceived by Professor Jan White and the Newham Early Years team, launched in 2015 and was an excellent example of how collaboration and commitment to research-led learning can transform practice. White's book *Every child a mover: A practical guide to providing young children with the physical opportunities they need* (Early Education, 2015) was an inspiration for and a key text during the Outdoors & Active programme. Twenty Newham Early Years settings worked collectively to explore ways of increasing physical activity in two- to four-year-olds, spending the best part of a year carrying out setting-based action research as well as attending a series of day-long CPD events.

Each CPD event was hosted by one of the participants, allowing the cohort to explore outdoor provision at other schools and settings – a hugely important research element that can be overlooked. The first day-long session focused on investigating the academic research that supports the notion of more vigorous and more frequent physical activity being good for young children's physical health and mental wellbeing. Movement specialist Jasmine Pasch shared insights into 'bodyfulness' and explained how different types of movement stimulate different parts of the child's brain and body. Case studies and evidence from visits to a wide range of settings helped illustrate the importance of physical, intellectual and emotional risk-taking in outdoor play.

The second CPD event was held shortly after the first and brought the whole cohort together again, this time to debate and agree individual action research projects. Having discussed their initial ideas with their own colleagues, project participants then shared their intentions with the whole Outdoors & Active group, allowing us to create 'mini-hubs' of practitioners with similar objectives (for example, using natural materials to encourage physical activity; providing more opportunities for physical risk-taking). They were then able to provide one another with specific peer support throughout the action research phase.

Between the second and third CPD events, participants worked in their settings, developing theories and testing them through tweaks to everyday provision. They would then reflect on the impact of these tweaks and develop or adapt them as necessary. As there are no 'right' or 'wrong' answers in action research, participants had the confidence to experiment and recognise that an unintended consequence or unwanted outcome genuinely was an opportunity for learning.

Backing up the focused work in settings, I visited every setting twice over the course of the project, providing specific advice and information about the potential for active outdoor play and nudging participants towards new approaches, techniques or resources that could help them achieve their action research goal. I also emailed regular 'newsletters' highlighting examples from the participating settings – I thought of these as 'carrot and stick' emails, celebrating progress whilst reminding everyone to keep testing, reflecting and adapting.

At the end-of-programme event, participants shared their principal learning outcomes from Outdoors & Active. Every setting had recorded increased physical activity in their children, and most had also seen corresponding increases in willingness to take risks. Participants felt they were more adventurous as practitioners and more confident in advocating for children's right to move. Whilst many had been familiar with the NHS's recommendation that young children should be physically active for at least 180 minutes a day (2011, 2019), at the start of the programme few understood the fundamental connection between movement and cognition. Marjorie Ouvry's seminal and very accessible book *Exercising muscles and minds* (2003, NCB) really helped the cohort understand and apply this knowledge. Researching and understanding this biological imperative – through reading, observations and action research – had the biggest impact on outcomes for our learner group and the children they worked with.

Researching the importance of outdoors – What's out there?
Research-informed practice outdoors uses evaluation cyclically. It not only records children's achievements, but notes the outdoor context for

learning and how this might influence those outcomes. The context outdoors obviously includes any resources used, but importantly, it also encompasses elements that are unique to the outdoor learning environment – air temperature and pockets of micro-climate; wind speed and type of wind (I think we all know what happens to children on gusty, blustery days!); cloud cover or sunshine; ambient sounds from the neighbourhood; how other children and adults present are moving around; the time of year and resultant light levels – to list just a few. This level of observation might seem daunting, over and above your standard approach, but even if you just 'record' it in your head, it will help you ask the question: 'Would this have looked different if ... it was summer/it had rained/more children were around/I had interacted more (or less)/we had more space ...?' That straightforward piece of 'reflection research' will, in turn, help shape children's experiences outdoors.

In order for research to be applied, the type of information and the way it's absorbed must be differentiated. While it's mostly valuable, it's not all easily digested!

- Theoretical and academic texts can be complex and challenging. It's impossible to read everything out there, so instead focus on a particular theme, learning outcome or concept, and read around that. Look for phrases or ideas that resonate and ask yourself: What would that look like in *my* setting?
- Blogs, magazine articles, YouTube videos and such like are wonderful motivators, particularly for outdoor learning and play, as they are usually created by people (including me!) who are full of joy for their area of expertise. Bite-sized chunks of qualitative research can bring quantitative concepts to life – but it's important to remember that anecdotes are not evidence, so apply critical reasoning to these sources and don't be carried away by their (my) enthusiasm.
- Capturing and creating your own experiences. In Early Years we are adept at recording and reporting children's progress. We are perhaps less ready to reflect and act on our own expertise.

A notebook or poster recording your own lightbulb moments is a super way of building your confidence as a researcher and trusting your own judgement as a practitioner.

- Practice-informed case studies and texts allow practitioners to pick out relevant approaches and try them out, knowing that someone else has already been successful. The Outdoors & Active handbook (Early Education) is a good example of how this works.

The most valuable messages I've absorbed and learned stem from my own 'real' experiences: researching what works through visits to schools and settings; talking to practitioners, teachers and other landscape designers and (importantly) watching them work; asking settings to test ideas for me; developing peer support networks (this could perhaps be social media's saving grace); and mentoring and being mentored. I have an unremitting desire to know what sparks delight and joy in children when they are outdoors, and I want to understand the impact of those emotions on other outcomes. Where possible, I like to reconnect with schools and settings I've worked with in the past and evaluate longitudinal outcomes with a view to influencing the shape and effectiveness of future projects.

The 'traditional' research – for example, reading academic texts or attending seminars – provides the knowledge to back up the demands I then make on practitioners when I ask them to begin what can be a very challenging process of change.

RESEARCH AND CHANGE

The work I do with schools and settings is rooted in embracing change; I might be encouraging a new way of managing or resourcing outdoors, introducing fresh approaches to delivering a curriculum outdoors or enabling the setting to implement major landscaping improvements. Like most educators, the 'plan, do, review' process is at the core of how I go about making change happen. More specifically, it's a process of change originally researched and developed by the UK's leading outdoor learning and play charity, Learning through Landscapes (www.ltl.org.uk):

- Where are we now? *Evaluate the factors affecting the way outdoors is currently used, managed and resourced: Who uses it? When? What for? Who cares for it?*
- Where do we want to be? *Identify aims and goals: What do we want children to be able to DO (note: not 'have') outdoors?*
- How will we get there? *What changes will be needed in order to achieve these outcomes? Who else could help us think about this?*
- Make the changes. *Carry out the project/action research/ landscaping.*
- Where are we now? *Evaluate how the changes have affected the way outdoors is currently used, managed and resourced.*

Learning through Landscapes as an organisation emerged from research (Adams, 1990) during the late 1980s into how UK school grounds were used, designed and managed. A few years later, one of its most important pieces of research, led by Wendy Titman, explored how the design of school grounds influenced children's behaviour. *Special places, special people: The hidden curriculum of school grounds* (1994) made the case for high-quality outdoor spaces for learning and play and built on previous research by Tina Bruce (1991), Robin Moore (1986) and many others to demonstrate that for children, the external spaces at school were of the utmost value. One quote, from a child in one of the research schools, struck me so forcefully that it has become something of a guiding philosophy:

The thing is, if somebody looked at this school and the playground with just plain cement they will think it's not much of a place. If it looked better they'd think it was a better school. But there's no money – there is for carpet but not for the playground. Maybe it's not the money. Maybe they think it's good enough for us.

Change must be informed by a deep understanding of *why* the change is being made and *how* it will make a difference – now – for these children. Despite the resonance of that child's comment, we can't be sentimental about the outdoor spaces children have access to; if the school grounds or gardens are not working hard enough to support outcomes for children, then they aren't 'good value'. That's why the first part of the change process is researching and reflecting on what outdoors offers now. Teachers and practitioners expect their classrooms and indoor spaces to 'work' for children 100 per cent of the time and will adapt, change, move and resource as needed. Outdoors should be no different – and children *do* know when 'their' outdoor spaces are not afforded the care and respect they deserve by the adults tasked with doing just that.

OUTDOOR RESEARCH – GAME CHANGERS

In addition to *Special Places, Special People* and the texts I've referenced throughout, a number of crucial pieces of research have influenced my approach to creating high-quality, high-value outdoor spaces for children. Each is accessible and applicable to Early Years outdoor spaces and I would recommend any or all of them to practitioners intent on creating truly effective, immersive outdoor spaces.

- In *The Nursery School* (2009), activist, author and Nursery School Head Margaret McMillan draws on her interest in the work of Froebel to highlight the links between poverty, health and wellbeing and makes the case for child-led, free-flowing indoor and outdoor learning.
- 7Cs – an informational guide to young children's outdoor play spaces (https://sala.ubc.ca/sites/sala.ubc.ca/files/documents/7Cs. pdf) explores the qualities that combine to create high-quality outdoor spaces. This research programme, led by Professor Susan Herrington, had the most profound impact on the way I evaluate and design Early Years outdoor spaces. (I wrote a series of articles about the 7Cs for *Nursery World* magazine, aimed at guiding settings through the process of evaluating their own outdoor spaces using this approach. See https://www.nurseryworld.co.uk/category/ practice-guides/the-7cs-approach-to-early-years-outdoor-space.)

- A Shared Vision and Values for Outdoor Play in the Early Years sets out a 'manifesto' for outdoors, asserting a series of non-negotiables for the places and spaces young children spend so much time in. (Free download here: https://www.plloutdoors.org.uk/ey-advice.)
- The International School Grounds Alliance was formed in 2010 and runs conferences every two years. I've been fortunate enough to attend some of these, and the opportunity to visit schools around the globe really does offer a fresh insight into childhood and outdoor play. In particular, experiencing the work of Grün Macht Schule (http://gruen-macht-schule.de) in Berlin and Ko Senda's Kindergartens in Japan (find case studies here: https://www.plloutdoors.org.uk/casestudies) has played a huge role in shaping my own understanding of what children need outdoors.

In planning this chapter, I spoke to several outdoor play specialists and collaborators to cultivate a wider sense of how research informs outdoor practice in the UK. Matt Robinson at Learning through Landscapes noted the importance of seeking out and maintaining relationships with academics whose research is likely to influence or be influenced by his own role in supporting outdoor learning and play in Scotland. Denise Grant, a Reception teacher in an Infant School, taps into support provided by Local Authority networks, but also pointed out that her experience working at my 'outdoors all day, every day' holiday playscheme has had a significant impact on her confidence in advocating for challenging outdoor learning at school. Landscape architect Felicity Robinson finds that delivering CPD to teachers and practitioners and visiting schools is the best way to keep abreast of the real issues schools are facing when taking learning and play outdoors.

I use research – in its many guises – to develop thinking, support reflection and enable better decision-making. Research backs up and strengthens our core professional convictions, and the more time I spend working outdoors with Early Years settings the more I see the benefits research tells us to expect happening in practice.

TOP TIPS

- Research can be presented in many forms: embrace them all. Blogs, case studies, Pinterest pages, magazine articles and such like are not just 'fluff' – they all help to formulate your own ideas and shape a vision for your outdoor space. Just make sure you back them up with the evidence-based research that 'makes the case' for better outdoor learning and play.
- Experience as many different settings as you practically can. I've found that schools and settings are generally delighted to be able to share what they do and how they do it. Observing children in contrasting environments to your own is absolutely crucial research if you plan to make changes to the way you use or manage outdoors. If visits are tricky, make use of the Siren Films (https://www.sirenfilms.co.uk/video-clip-library-early-years-training/) video clip library, which is an excellent source of evidence.
- Action research is effective and enjoyable and fits into a normal working pattern. The first step is to simply be more aware 'in the moment' of your own interactions (Fisher, 2016) so that you learn to recognise the consequences your decisions have on outcomes and can shape them accordingly.

REFERENCES

Adams, E. (1990). *Report on the use, design, management and development of school grounds*. Crediton: Southgate Publishers.

Bruce, T. (1991). *Time to play in early childhood education*. London: Hodder and Stoughton.

Early Education. Outdoors and active. Retrieved from https://www.early-education.org.uk/outdoorsandactive.

Fisher, J. (2016). *Interacting or interfering? Improving interactions in the early years*. Oxford: OUP.

Learning through Landscapes. Retrieved from https://www.ltl.org.uk/.

McMillan, M. (2019). *The nursery school*. London: Forgotten Books.

Moore, R. C. (1986). *Childhood's domain – Play and place in child development*. London: Croom Helm Ltd.

Mountain, J. The 7Cs approach to Early Years outdoor space, *Nursery World*. Retrieved from https://www.nurseryworld.co.uk/category/practice-guides/the-7cs-approach-to-early-years-outdoor-space.

NHS (2011). Physical activity guidelines for early years – For children who are capable of walking. Factsheet. Retrieved from https://www.nhs.uk/Livewell/fitness/Documents/children-under-5-walking.pdf. Similar documents are available for non-walking under 5s.

NHS (page last reviewed 2019). Physical activity guidelines for children (under 5 years). Retrieved from https://www.nhs.uk/live-well/exercise/physical-activity-guidelines-children-under-five-years/.

Ouvry, M. (2003). *Exercising muscles and minds*. London: National Children's Bureau. A second edition is now available: ISBN 978-1785922664 (Ouvry, M. and Furtado, A. (2020). London: Jessica Kingsley Publishers.)

Peters, J. (2004). Teachers engaging in action research: challenging some assumptions, *Educational Action Research* 12(4), 535–556.

Titman, W. (1994). *Special places, special people: The hidden curriculum of school grounds*. WWF/Southgate Publishers.

White, J. (2015). *Every child a mover: A practical guide to providing young children with the physical opportunities they need*. Early Education.

ENGLAND'S SUMMER-BORN CHILDREN: AN EQUITABLE EDUCATION?

A CASE STUDY FROM A SMALL FEDERATION OF THREE INFANT SCHOOLS

JANE FLOOD

Jane Flood is a Head of Learning at a small infant school in England and also a part-time PhD candidate at Durham University, studying how teachers use research to inform their practice.

MATT PERRETT

Matt Perrett is a Senior Teacher in a small first school in Somerset. He is currently undertaking the NPQSL (National Professional Qualification for Senior Leadership) and is an SLE (a Specialist Leader of Education) for the Early Years.

Matt and Jane worked together at a federation of infant schools in Hampshire.

Virtually all education systems have a single cut-off date that determines when children become eligible for compulsory schooling, and studies have shown that age on school entry is an important determinant of early pupil achievement (Balestra et al., 2020; Institute for Fiscal Studies, 2010). In England children start formal schooling during the September after they turn four, where a school year runs from September to July. Children join the Early Years Foundation Stage (EYFS) class. The term 'summer-born' is used to refer to children born from 1 April to 31 August (Long, 2015), making children born then the youngest in their school year and so developmentally some months behind the oldest. Parents can apply to admission authorities to defer school entry if they feel their child is not ready to start school before compulsory school age (the prescribed days of 31 December, 31 March or 31 August following a child's fifth birthday) or they can choose to send their child part-time until this date. Numerous studies report that month of birth matters to summer-born children's educational attainment (Adams, 2015; Everett, 2015; Long, 2015; Mitchell, 2019), with younger children performing significantly worse than older peers in tests (Long, 2015). According to the Institute for Fiscal Studies (2013, p. 4), 'these differences arise purely as a result of the organisation of the education system; there is nothing fundamentally different about August born children'. As a group of EYFS practitioners, we felt the system was disadvantaging the children rather than the children being fundamentally different. We were keen to investigate this further and explore ways to give some balance back to the youngest children.

Yet the plight of summer-born children has yet to be addressed in education policy terms. Since 2010, government policy in England has focused on children acquiring essential 'knowledge and concepts', leading to a skills-based curriculum favouring literacy, maths and science rather than a broad and balanced curriculum. This education policy agenda has resulted in a perceived top-down pressure on Early Years settings (Early Education, 2018) to become more like formal schooling, resulting in Reception classes being praised for building their curriculums around literacy and maths and resulting in 30 four- and five-year-olds being exposed to formal learning earlier and earlier.

Teachers and school leaders are pressurised by a school readiness narrative and a focus in schools on testing. In a study of three primary academies in England, Mitchell et al. (2019) concluded that teachers viewed their class as a whole cohort, without the necessary differentiation needed for an equitable education for the youngest children, driven by a focus on the acquisition of literacy and numeracy skills. On entry in September, all children undertake a government-mandated baseline test as part of the accountability measures used to judge schools' performance. At the end of a child's EYFS year in school, teacher assessment is used to track which children have reached a 'good level of development' against the 17 Early Learning Goals (ELGs). This is reported to parents and the Department for Education (DfE) after moderation locally by Local Education Authorities. The current school system in England means that measurement against end of year ELGs gives significant advantage (developmentally and emotionally) to those children born in September over their summer-born classmates, especially those born in August. There is some evidence that this pattern continues through education – by the age of seven, September-born children are three times more likely to be in the top stream than August-born children (Centre for Longitudinal Studies, 2013). Viewing the autumn- and summer-born children through the same lens, without differentiation, leads to equity issues (Mitchell, 2019) and is contrary to the DfE's statement: 'Every child is a unique child' (Early Years Foundation Stage, 2017).

Although children are ready to learn at all ages, young children are usually less prepared to engage in academic or formal work than their peers; this is the developmental disadvantage of the summer-born children (Balestra, 2019). Summer-born children can suffer serious educational disadvantage because they are less physically, socially and emotionally ready for school compared with typical Reception classes. Studies have shown the non-academic effects of being summer-born; younger children feature significantly higher on SEN (special educational needs) registers (Long, 2015), especially with behavioural problems or speech and language delay (Balestra et al., 2019), than their older peers; they are often placed in low-ability groups, which can reinforce the disadvantage of being summer-born (Centre for Longitudinal Studies, 2013), and can suffer from mental health issues through low self-esteem and low confidence in their own abilities (Mitchell, 2019).

Working in a Federation of 3 small infant schools in the south of England, the EYFS team comprised 2 full-time teachers, 2 part-time teachers and 5 TAs (teaching assistants) working with 90 children on this project. As a result of our demographic, there is pressure to ensure more than 80 per cent of each class of 30 four- and five-year-olds make a good level of development (GLD) against 17 ELGs in July each year. This can overshadow the diverse needs of the youngest children in our classes and can be at odds with developing a play-based curriculum recognised as essential for young children's development (Moyles, 2015; UNICEF, 2018). In 2015 we took part in a Research Learning Community (RLC) project (Rose et al., 2017), facilitated by our local Teaching School and supported by Professor Chris Brown; RLCs promote the use of knowledge from research and practitioner knowledge, with both of equal value in the process (Brown 2015, 2016). To put it simply, teachers learn from and build on existing academic knowledge to develop new and effective innovations to improve pupil outcomes. Fundamental to this approach is the support of school leadership (Brown, 2015). Promoting the principles of RLCs, and in keeping with factors identified by Brown and Zhang (2016) of teachers using research-informed enquiry to trial and evaluate the impact of new classroom approaches, a cycle of enquiry began focused on reducing the gap in attainment of our summer-born children in writing. An analysis of our 2014 end of year data showed that typically summer-born children were not attaining the end of year expectations, especially in writing, compared with other ELGs and with their older peers. For example, in 2014 60 per cent of the children in the federation (3 Reception classes) achieved their ELG for writing compared with 67 per cent of age equivalent children across the Local Authority and 83 per cent of their older peers across the federation.

Starting with the end in mind (Stoll, 2015), the aim of the project was for a more equitable outcome for our summer-born children, with a focus on writing without compromising our commitment to a play-based curriculum or formalising our provision. In the first year we made a number of positive changes to our teaching practice, classroom organisation and systems for moving from parental involvement towards parental engagement in their children's learning (Goodall and Montgomery, 2014). Developing research-informed teaching strategies required us to start by looking at the evidence in professional journals and books and discussing this in relation to our own professional expertise within the EYFS team. Teachers' access to pertinent research can be a barrier to research-informed practice, but in this case our involvement with the RLC through the Teaching School meant Professor Brown could support us and ensure the credibility of the research we were accessing. Since then, the Chartered College of Teaching, the Research Schools Network and organisations such as the EEF (Education Endowment Fund) can provide research and research summaries to teachers.

Through many professional learning conversations in the EYFS team, we developed a different pedagogical model for the youngest children. For example, we provided a variety of meaningful writing opportunities linked to the children's interests to develop a positive attitude about themselves as writers and to practise writing independently during child-initiated learning. This was individual to each child, taking into account their current skill level and their developmental next steps, and was particularly relevant for the summer-born children, whose needs could differ significantly from typical EYFS norms. The children quickly became aware of the value the adults were placing on their independent 'writing', and their confidence and enthusiasm flourished. This confidence was supported by the skills taught in adult-directed groups, with an emphasis on saying, recognising and recording letters (i.e. phonics), starting earlier than previously (during the first weeks in school) in mixed-ability small groups. The recording element here rarely involved paper and pencils but a variety of media (chalks, paint, chunky pens, water, etc.) on vertical and horizontal surfaces inside and outside the classroom designed to support gross and fine motor development of all children. At the same time, the classroom space was reorganised to promote writing everywhere through constantly changing enhanced provision matched to children's changing interests and skills.

Parental engagement was an essential aspect of this project. Borrowing from the work of Janet Goodall (2017), this was a deliberate move to involve parents actively as partners in their children's learning compared with just being involved in school life. A series of family workshops organised in the first few weeks of the children starting school involved parents or family members coming into school for six 1-hour group sessions to work alongside their child and teacher. In the first parent–child session – before the children arrived – we explained about the project and explained the plight of summer-born children in England's education system. These sessions helped parents have a better understanding of the work we were doing with the youngest children in school, how this could help the children develop early writing skills (the focus of the project) and how they could support their child at home. This first session ensured that parents understood our focus was on term of birth rather than their children being chosen following any assessment. The parent feedback helped us to gain a greater insight into individual children's learning behaviours, make more accurate assessments and reflect on the project as it progressed. We promoted the idea quoted earlier that summer-born children are not fundamentally different to their older peers and could benefit from a 'little and often' approach involving lots of play-based experiences to maintain confidence and self-belief rather than portraying them as 'catching up' or 'behind'. It also helped mitigate the parents' perceived 'failure' of their summer-born child at the end of their first year in school, gave the parents an insight into how their child was actually doing alongside peers of the same age and helped develop the children's confidence as writers starting from wherever they were.

Teachers gained confidence in seeing the summer-born children as individuals with differentiated expectations, not as part of a cohort or class focused on the acquisition of literacy skills (Mitchell, 2019). Professional learning conversations (Brown, 2015) amongst the EYFS team and school leaders soon revealed that, with high-quality teaching and increased parental engagement, summer-born children could master the mechanics of writing in ways that were appropriate to their emotional and social maturity. Teachers gained further professional knowledge through joint professional development (JPD) activities such as visiting other schools and settings and seminars with Professor Brown. By the end of the year, through evaluating the cycle of enquiry, teachers could clearly articulate a Theory of Action (Figure 1) (a 'route map' that steered the teachers towards their intended outcome for the summer-born project) (Flood & Brown, 2017) to improve the writing attainment of summer-born children.

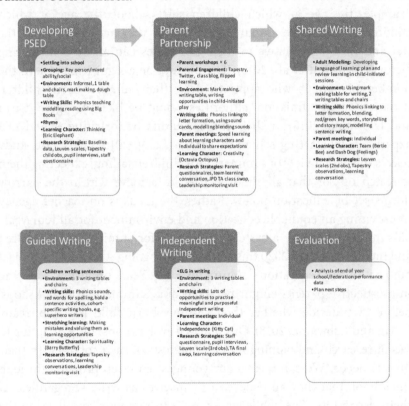

Figure 1: A Theory of Action:
Closing the gap for summer-born children in writing

Scrutiny of end of first year data showed an increase in summer-born children achieving end of year expectations in writing, with an increase from 60 per cent at the end of 2014 to 86 per cent at the end of 2015. The RLC project continued the following year, with teachers developing the intervention further to develop summer-born children's learning behaviours more generally and a focus on improved staff interactions during child-initiated play.

A single solution may not address all the factors associated with summer-born children attaining less well than their older peers. For example, the age at which children start school, the age at which children sit tests, the amount of schooling they receive prior to the test and their age relative to their classmates can all be contributing factors (Crawford et al., 2013). There could be a significant rise in the number of parents who apply to defer their summer-born children if they thought admission authorities would be likely to agree (Cirin and Lubwama, 2018) or their child wouldn't be forfeiting their EYFS experience by starting school in Year 1 (Long, 2015). This case study rejects the deficit view of summer-born children failing, expecting them to 'catch up', or that all children need to achieve within the narrow norms set by education policy. Rather, the focus is on teacher agency in providing an equitable education and environment for all four-year-olds, underpinned by a system of support for summer-born children and their families. In 2020 this work is still ongoing – no longer a project but part of the Federation's culture for Early Years provision, resulting in prospective parents enquiring about our 'Summer-born workshops' before they decide whether their summer-born child is school ready (Cirin and Lubwama, 2018). Our practice evolves constantly, adapting to recent research and tapping into the interests of each cohort with their diverse needs. We can see, as our youngest children progress through the school, that they all believe in themselves as writers, regardless of their test results. The challenge for us is to maintain and develop the principles learned from research and how this theory of action evolved. As teachers and school leaders change in our Federation, we need to make sure our youngest children, 'the summer-borns', are given the education they deserve.

TOP TIPS

- Parental Engagement – involve parents in the project from the outset and be open and honest about the need for the focus on the youngest children.
- Ensure leadership commitment to the project, ensuring the time and resources are committed for the project to succeed.
- Keep a research log – tracking the Theory of Action as the project evolves, developing professional learning conversations involving all the team.

REFERENCES

Adams, R. (4 June 2015). Summer born children in danger of being left behind, says school study, *The Guardian*. Retrieved from https://www.theguardian.com/education/2015/jun/04/summer-born-children-left-behind-in-the-classroom-says-study.

Balestra, S., Eugster, B. and Liebert, H. (2020). Summer-born struggle: The effect of school starting age on health, education, and work, *Health Economics* 29, 591–607.

Brown, C. (ed.) (2015). *Leading the use of research & evidence in schools*. London: IOE Press.

Brown, C. (2016). Changing practice: the power of Research Learning Communities, *Professional Development Today* 18(4), 56–66.

Brown, C. & Zhang, D. (2016). How can school leaders establish evidence-informed schools: An analysis of the effectiveness of potential school policy levers, *Educational Management and Leadership* 45(3), 382–401.

Campbell, T. (2013). In-school ability grouping and the month of birth effect, *Centre for Longitudinal Studies*. London: IOE. Retrieved from https://cls.ucl.ac.uk/wp-content/uploads/2017/04/Ability-grouping-and-the-month-of-birth-effect-T-Campbell-March-2013-FINAL.pdf.

Cirin, R. and Lubwama, J. (2018). *Delayed school admissions for summer born pupils. Research Report. Department for Education*. Retrieved from https://assets.publishing.service.gov.uk/government/uploads/system/uploads/attachment_data/file/833610/Delayed_school_admissions_for_summer-born_pupils.pdf.

Crawford, C., Dearden, L. and Greaves, E. (2013). *When you are born matters: Evidence for England*. London (Institute for Fiscal Studies Report R80). Retrieved from https://www.ifs.org.uk/comms/r80.pdf.

Department for Education (2012). *Development Matters in the Early Years Foundation stage (EYFS)*. Retrieved from https://www.foundationyears.org.uk/files/2012/03/Development-Matters-FINAL-PRINT-AMENDED.pdf.

Early Education (2018). What's wrong with Ofsted's Bold Beginnings report? The British Association for Early Childhood Education, 30 January, 2018. Retrieved from https://www.early-education.org.uk/news/whats-wrong-ofsteds-bold-beginnings-report.

Everett, F. (9 September 2015). Why summer born children are scarred for life, *The Telegraph*. Retrieved from https://www.telegraph.co.uk/education/educationopinion/11853803/Why-summer-born-children-are-scarred-for-life.html.

Flood, J. and Brown, C. (2018). Does a theory of action approach help teachers engage in evidence-informed self-improvement?', *Research for All* 2(2), 347–358.

Goodall, J. (2017). *Narrowing the achievement gap: Parental engagement in children's learning*. London: Routledge.

Goodall, J. and Montgomery, C. (2014). Parental involvement to parental engagement: A continuum, *Educational Review* 66(4), 399–410.

House of Commons Briefing paper (2015), Long, R. Summer born children: starting school (No 07272), London.

Mitchell, E. (2019). A small-scale exploratory study of educator's perceptions and expectations of summer-born children in the reception classes of three English primary academies and the strategies used to support them, *Education 3–13* 47(2), 205–216.

Moyles, J. (2015). *The Excellence of Play*. United Kingdom: Open University Press.

Rose, J., Thomas, S., Zhang, L., Edwards, A., Augero, A. and Roney, P. (2017). *Research Learning Communities Evaluation*. Education Endowment Foundation.

Stoll, L. and Brown, C. (2015). Middle leaders as catalysts for evidence-informed change. In C. Brown (ed.), *Leading the use of research & evidence in schools*. London: IOE Press.

UNICEF (2018). Learning though play: Strengthening learning through play in early childhood education programmes. Retrieved from https://www.unicef.org/sites/default/files/2018-12/UNICEF-Lego-Foundation-Learning-through-Play.pdf.

UNLOCKING RESEARCH: PARENTAL ENGAGEMENT IN CHILDREN'S LEARNING
PREPARING TO TAKE RESEARCH INTO PRACTICE

JANET GOODALL

Janet Goodall (EdD) is an associate professor in the School of Education at Swansea University. Her main area of research is family and parental engagement in young people's learning. She has researched, written and lectured widely on this topic, working with schools, families, local authorities and charitable bodies in the UK and further afield. Her most recent book, co-authored with Dr Kathryn Weston, *100 ideas for secondary teachers: engaging parents*, follows on from their previous book, *100 ideas for primary teachers: engaging parents*, both available from Bloomsbury Education.

Before we go any further, I'd like you to answer honestly – just to yourself but as honestly as you can – the following question: Are you willing, really willing, to change your practice based on what you find in the research? If the answer is yes, then please carry on. If the answer is, it depends on the research, fair enough, but be sure that your criteria for use are about the validity of the research, not your own comfort zone. If the answer is no, then there's not much point in reading any further.

The question is not an idle one, and it is one to which we will return; but the important point is made: allowing one's practice to become research-informed means being able and willing to change that practice based on the outcomes of research.

As this chapter moves on, I'll discuss (briefly) what the research says about parental engagement in children's learning. ('Parents' here should be taken to include parents, and any other adult with a significant caring responsibility for the child in question.) This section is fairly brief, because although the research base is wide and varied, the messages are fairly straightforward. I will then go on to talk about becoming research-informed, and look at what research-informed practice around parental engagement with learning might look like. I will give some very brief suggestions about instances of practice (you don't really need these, as the rest of the chapter should set you up to devise your own practices) and will end with a final, supporting statement and some tips to consider.

PARENTAL ENGAGEMENT IN CHILDREN'S LEARNING

It has become a truism of much of the literature around schooling that parental engagement in learning is a vital part of narrowing the achievement gap between children from different backgrounds (Fan and Chen, 2001; Jeynes, 2007; Jeynes, 2012; Goodall, 2017), and for good reasons. Parental engagement with children's learning can lead to a wide range of improvements, such as increases in homework return rates, reductions in absenteeism and increased outcomes for students (O'Mara et al., 2010; Berkowitz et al., 2017; Wood and Bauman, 2017).

WHAT PARENTAL ENGAGEMENT IS/IS NOT

It is important to be clear about what is meant by 'parental engagement in children's learning'. The literature and experience show that there is often a confusion among school staff between parental involvement in school and schooling, and parental engagement in learning. As with any discussion, it's important to define terms at the outset, especially with a term so often misunderstood as parental engagement with learning. I take the term to mean parents' interest in and support for learning.

Parental involvement in school and schooling (Goodall and Montgomery, 2013) is focused on the school, and it remains the domain of teaching staff. Agency continues to rest with school staff, and parents are perceived as 'helping' teachers, who are considered to be the only real authorities on learning and education (Berkowitz et al., 2017; Goodall, 2017). This model is school-centric, that is, it is focused on the school rather than on learning (or, indeed, on the child).

However, the effective elements of parental engagement take place not at school, but rather in what has been called the 'home learning environment' (Desforges and Abouchaar, 2003; Sylva et al., 2004). Such engagement with learning does not require parents to deliver school-based content (Goodall, 2020); rather, it is vested in attitudes toward learning, conversations (OECD, 2012) and supportive forms of parenting. This form of engagement is focused on learning rather than on the school. The beneficiary of the process is the child, whose learning is supported (rather than the school, which is 'helped' by parents).

The move toward support for authentic parental engagement with learning is hampered in many schools, and indeed systems, by deficit modes of thought surrounding parents (Goodall, 2019). Within this model, parents are often seen as being in need of help – that is, school staff must supply what is lacking for parents and families (Valencia, 2010; Valencia, 2012; Baquedano-López et al., 2013). I'm going to suggest that you do *not* proceed from this standpoint, because the research shows that it's not as effective as working from an asset-based approach.

THE GAP BETWEEN RESEARCH AND PRACTICE

It may seem odd to talk about moving to research-informed practice around parental engagement in the Early Years – don't Early Years practitioners already do this better than the rest of the formal schooling sector?

In my experience the answer to that question is yes, they do; in fact, I've often suggested that colleagues from secondaries go and speak to their Early Years counterparts on just this subject.

This doesn't mean, however, that there is nothing left for practitioners in the Early Years to learn, particularly from each other.

That leads me to the first point I'd like to make – or rather, myth I'd like to dispel.

WHO DOES THE INFORMING, IN RESEARCH-INFORMED PRACTICE?

There is, at times, a backlash against educational research as coming from 'the outside', meaning that researchers are not at the chalk (or whiteboard) face every day. Yet a closer look at most research, particularly on parental engagement with learning, shows that it is very firmly placed on the inside, that it, it's taking place in settings and schools themselves. Becoming 'research-informed' is a way of learning from a wider pool of practitioners and colleagues than might otherwise be available. This is particularly the case with the rise of practitioner-led research (teacher research, action research, etc.).

So, being 'research-informed' means learning from peers across a very wide range – around the world, in fact – as well as taking part in organised training opportunities and individual reading. It means being aware – selectively, critically aware – of what's going on, and what you can learn from others. This process is a valid form of professional development and should be recognised as such.

BEING SELECTIVELY INFORMED: OVERCOMING THE BARRIERS

I've referred to being 'selectively informed', and for a good reason.

There are barriers practitioners face in integrating research into practice, particularly around a concept that may seem as nebulous (and often as ill-defined) as parental engagement. These barriers may be summed up as 'time', 'access' and 'integration'.

Time

It's very difficult for any teacher to find the time to engage with research; in fact, I'd say it's impossible – if you go looking for the time, you won't find it. Rather, time must be made, which means becoming research-informed has to be a deliberate process and given priority among all the other calls on a teacher's time. Using research to inform your practice is not an additional, optional extra to be slotted in when there's a gap (because let's be honest, there's never a gap). Rather, it's part of being a professional; continual updating of knowledge and skills is part of what it means for something to be a profession. To find time to read, digest and incorporate the literature into practice requires actively scheduling the time needed to do that. This is a legitimate part of any professional's role and is an important (though often unrecognised) part of continuing professional development.

Access

While not often mentioned in discussions of research-informed practice, *accessing the research* can be an unexpectedly difficult barrier to surmount.

Access covers two areas: finding appropriate research and then getting hold of it.

Finding appropriate literature can be a challenge in itself, and it's worth taking the time to find out how to make Google Scholar (probably the most accessible search engine for this kind of thing) work for you. Take some time to learn how to narrow down results to items that are useful to use.

But having found an article or report is only the first part of the process; often the second part seems more difficult, as you may be presented with paywalls, with websites demanding payment for the items you want to read.

There are a number of things to try here, assuming you don't have the ready funds to be able to access everything you want. If you are a member of the Chartered College of Teachers, you may have access to articles through that body. If the author is at a UK university, there's a good chance that some version of the paper will be accessible through their institutional website (e.g. Swansea University). This may be a Word document of the author's final copy rather than the version published in the journal, but will be essentially the same and hold the same information. (Academics who are subject to the Research Excellence Framework have to make papers submitted to that process open access in one form or another. As this mainly covers the period from 2014 to the end of 2020, that may limit the scope of papers available, but it's still worth a try and easily done.) If all else fails, it's worth writing to the author (their details will often be available with the abstract to the piece). Most of us are thrilled to know anyone is reading our work, and the author may be able to share a copy of the paper with you, depending on the terms agreed with journals, etc.

(While I've mentioned narrowing your search terms, and that's a necessary part of the process, don't narrow your sights too much. Being research-informed, as I've mentioned, means being willing to change, and that means at times venturing into the unknown).

Integration

The final barrier to research-informed practice is inherent in the name, and relates to that question I asked at the outset – having found and read and absorbed the research, what impact will it have on your day-to-day teaching? What impact *will you allow it to have* on your practice? The point of the exercise is not to (just) be informed about the research, but to allow, or to ensure, that the outcomes of research have an impact on your day-to-day practice.

This is often the least obvious but most insurmountable of barriers, because it strikes so close to home. Most of us think we're good at what we do, so accepting that we need to change – and perhaps to change profoundly – can be very hard to do.

WHAT WOULD CHANGE IF YOU LET THE RESEARCH AROUND PARENTAL ENGAGEMENT WITH CHILDREN'S LEARNING IMPACT ON YOUR PRACTICE?

It would be an asset-based approach

I have listed this change as the first because it is the most important. It would be entirely possible to implement all the other changes in this section, and indeed much of the research, from the more common deficit-based approach to parents and parental engagement (Lapierre, 2008; Valencia, 2012; Goodall, 2019), and changes implemented in this way are still likely to have some beneficial outcomes. I believe, however, it would be a misnomer to call such superficial changes truly research-informed. Research related, perhaps, but not informed. Practice that is truly informed by research in this area would start from a wholesale re-understanding of the place of parents (and schools) in young people's learning.

Simply put, asset-based practice around parental engagement with learning sees parents as partners in young people's learning. It actually puts into practice phrases one hears but rarely observes, as it were, in the wild, acknowledging and acting on the belief that parents are integral to learning.

The opposite approach is all too easy to spot (both in the wild and in policy rhetoric). A deficit approach to parental engagement sees professional teachers as the only teachers, confuses learning overall with the subset of learning that is encased in schooling (Goodall, 2017) and acts on the premise that teachers should be in charge of all areas of learning. Parents are useful, of course, even within this understanding, but they are very much second-tier players and should play only as directed by teachers. Their role is to support teachers or the school as a whole.

Moving from this deficit approach to an asset approach is actually a profound change in the understanding of the role of parents, even in the Early Years sector, which often interacts with parents on a far more regular basis than colleagues in the secondary sector, for example. This change – this element of being research-informed – may seem to strike at much of what lies at the heart of the profession and professionalism. It supports, however, what is and always has been the central aim of teaching: to facilitate learning, and to do so as well as possible for all young people.

The research is clear that parental support of learning in the home is of value, regardless of who the parents are or what their background may be (Sylva et al., 2008). This concept mitigates against a deficit view of 'those' parents – whoever may be covered by that pronoun. Parents from all sorts of backgrounds and educational levels are able to support learning at home (Jeynes, 2012; Jeynes, 2014; Punter et al., 2016; Roy and Giraldo-García, 2018).

The chances are high that this is not the view you were taught to take of parents in your training (Tett, 2001; Mandarakas, 2014; Thompson et al., 2018; Willemse et al., 2018), or have encountered afterwards during your career. This is why I asked if you were willing to change, and to accept profound change to practice, which is based on a change of fairly embedded beliefs.

The move to an asset-based view of parents will not happen quickly or without work; you will be, in many ways, unlearning much of what you have been taught and probably come to believe about the place of parents in relation to schools and schooling. As I've mentioned, it would be possible to undertake the rest of the changes suggested here without this first, fundamental rethinking, but it will be much easier and far more effective to enact further changes from an asset-based view of parental engagement.

RESEARCH-INFORMED PRACTICE AROUND PARENTAL ENGAGEMENT WOULD CENTRE ON LEARNING, NOT ON THE SCHOOL (OR THE TEACHER)

A caveat is necessary here: I'm talking about (and the research talks about) learning as a process rather than learning as solely content or that-which-is-to-be-learned.

One of the more important aspects of parental engagement with children's learning is the attitude toward learning that is present in the home (Harris and Goodall, 2008). You are probably aware of the importance of mastery orientations to learning – learning for the sake of learning – for young people (Pomerantz et al., 2006; Puklek Levpušček and Zupančič, 2009; Goodall, 2020). This is something you can usefully share with parents, along with all the ways you support self-efficacy among your pupils every day.

This element of research-informed practice would entail sharing ideas with parents about work to do at home that is aimed at supporting self-efficacy (rather than busy work or completion of school-based tasks). It would *also* entail *listening* to parents – what they can tell you about their children, and about how the family supports learning at home – and being open to ways of supporting learning that had not previously occurred to you. (One way of beginning these conversations, particularly in the Early Years, is simply to ask parents why they chose a particular name for their child, which can open discussions into families' backgrounds, history, etc.).

This is more of an attitudinal change than a set of specific practices. But a changed attitude – based on the research showing the value of the home learning environment – will allow you to create specific practices that are appropriate in your situation. This brings me to the final category of research-informed practice around parental engagement.

RESEARCH-INFORMED PRACTICE AROUND PARENTAL ENGAGEMENT WITH CHILDREN'S LEARNING IS FLEXIBLE, ADAPTABLE AND SENSITIVE

You may have noticed there are precious few actual practices mentioned in this article, very few 'tips' that you can pick up and just use. I've explained why this should be the case, but the final piece of the puzzle is this: whatever you do must be appropriate for the families you work with (Goodall and Vorhaus, 2011).

That means, of course, that you need to know and understand those families – you need to know, for example, what languages they speak at home (and the attitudinal change mentioned above means seeing additional languages *as an asset*, not a deficit), and what their hopes and dreams are for their children. This means you need to listen to them – schools and school staff are remarkably good at giving information to parents, but think about it – you don't teach simply by giving children information (you know better than that), so how can that be an appropriate way of supporting learning in the home (Goodall, 2017)?

RESEARCH-INFORMED PRACTICE(S)

It seems unfair to end this chapter without giving some examples of what such practices might be, but I do so with the caveat that you must, as above, adapt these to your situation. I have few worries about that process: teachers are past masters at adapting things; it's *the attitude with which they are adapted* that matters.

- Report the good as well as the bad. This may seem obvious and, indeed, it is much more engrained in Early Years practice than other phases of education, but please don't neglect to tell parents the good things, the funny and heart-warming things, as well as the problematic things.

- Keep records of interactions with parents – you may find that there are parents you never spend any time with simply because 'there's no reason to' – their child is doing well; there are no issues. That doesn't mean, however, that these parents don't need support or even to be told that you can see the results of their good work! (Goodall and Weston, 2018)
- Prepare questions for both parents and staff for parents' evening. We all know what these meetings are like – hurried and often deeply unsatisfying. Make them, instead, a chance to discuss the child and their learning; suggest to parents that they come prepared to ask how they can support learning, *and to staff* that they come to the meeting prepared to ask parents to tell them something about the child that will help the teacher help them to learn (Goodall, 2016; Goodall, 2018).
- Ban 'hard to reach' (Goodall and Weston, 2018). I don't mean ban parents or families – I mean ban the phrase and all other phrases that show deficit views of parents. Instead, think about why parents might be hard to reach and remember – the important thing is not that they interact with you but that they interact with their child's learning.
- Share something about yourself – and, with permission, about other members of staff – with parents. One way of doing this is simple and fun: add photos of staff and their pets to the school website. It can be an instant link with families (Goodall and Weston, 2018).

These are just a few tips, but you'll be able to think of many, many more once you've had a chance to really think through what approaching parents from an asset-based view really looks like.

And that brings me to:

A FINAL SUPPORTING STATEMENT

There's very little in this chapter that you don't already know how to do and probably practice every working day, simply because you (I hope) approach your students from an asset framework – what *can* they do; how can you support them to go further?

You have the skills; you know how to support learning.

What the research is asking you to do is to extend those skills to working with parents.

TOP TIPS

These tips need to be understood in light of the rest of this chapter, that is – they are part of an overall process rather than ideas that stand on their own. With that understanding, may I offer:

- Read widely – and perhaps wildly. Read beyond the confines of what is suggested to you. Read things you're going to disagree with, but formulate your arguments as to *why* you disagree – and base these on evidence as well. You'll find this is an iterative (and virtuous) circle.
- Write. Write short precis of what you've read, write a response, write a blog post, write an essay (do a further degree and write a thesis!). Reading is good, but reading and thinking is much, much better, and putting your ideas into words and onto paper is a useful part of that process. You can share your writing (blog post) or keep it entirely private – the purpose is to enhance your thinking.
- Let part of that writing be a research-into-practice diary. What do you *want* to change, based on the research? (Note the actions and the source). What *have* you changed as a result of the research? And most importantly, what *impact* has that change had?

These three all go together and are designed to help you really have practice that is research-informed. Good luck!

REFERENCES

Baquedano-López, P., Alexander, R. A. and Hernández, S. J. (2013). Equity issues in parental and community involvement in schools: What teacher educators need to know, *Review of Research in Education* 37(1), 149–182.

Berkowitz, R., Astor, R. A., Pineda, D., DePedro, K. T., Weiss, E. L. and Benbenishty, R. (2017). Parental involvement and perceptions of school climate in California, *Urban Education*. DOI: 0042085916685764.

Desforges, C. and Abouchaar, A. (2003). The impact of parental involvement, parental support and family education on pupil achievement and adjustment: A literature review. London: Department of Education and Skills.

Fan, X. and Chen, M. (2001). Parental involvement and students' academic achievement: A meta-analysis, *Educational Psychology Review* 13(1), 1–22.

Goodall, J. (2016). Parental Engagement Toolkit, Wiltshire Pilot.

Goodall, J. (2017). Learning-centred parental engagement: Freire reimagined, *Educational Review* 70(5), 1–19.

Goodall, J. (2017). *Narrowing the achievement gap: Parental engagement with children's learning*. London: Routledge.

Goodall, J. (2018). A toolkit for parental engagement: From project to process, *School Leadership & Management* 38(2), 222–238.

Goodall, J. (2019). Parental engagement and deficit discourses: Absolving the system and solving parents, *Educational Review*, 1–13.

Goodall, J. (2020). Scaffolding homework for mastery: Engaging parents, *Educational Review*, 1–21.

Goodall, J. and Montgomery, C. (2013). Parental involvement to parental engagement: A continuum, *Educational Review* 66(4), 399–410.

Goodall, J. and Vorhaus, J. (2011). Review of best practice in parental engagement. London: Department of Education.

Goodall, J. and Weston, K. (2018). *100 Ideas for Primary Teachers: Engaging Parents*. London: Bloomsbury.

Harris, A. and Goodall, J. (2008). Do parents know they matter? Engaging all parents in learning, *Educational Research* 50(3), 277–289.

Jeynes, W. (2012). 'A meta-analysis of the efficacy of different types of parental involvement programs for urban students, *Urban Education* 47(4), 706–742.

Jeynes, W. H. (2007). The relationship between parental involvement and urban secondary school student academic achievement: A meta-analysis, *Urban Education* 42(1), 82–110.

Jeynes, W. H. (2014). Parental involvement that works... because it's age-appropriate, *Kappa Delta Pi Record* 50(2), 85–88.

Lapierre, S. (2008). Mothering in the context of domestic violence: The pervasiveness of a deficit model of mothering, *Child & Family Social Work* 13(4), 454–463.

Mandarakas, M. (2014). Teachers and parent—school engagement: International perspectives on teachers' preparation for and views about working with parents, *Global Studies of Childhood* 4(1), 21–27.

O'Mara, A., Jamal, F., Llewellyn, A., Lehmann, A., Cooper, C. and Bergeron, C. (2010). Improving children's and young people's outcomes through support for mothers, fathers, and carers, C4EO.

OECD (2012). PISA – Let's read them a story! The Parent Factor in Education, OECD Publishing.

Puklek Levpušček, M. and Zupančič, M. (2009). Math achievement in early adolescence: The role of parental involvement, teachers' behavior, and students' motivational beliefs about math, *Journal of Early Adolescence* 29(4), 541–570.

Pomerantz, E. M., Ng, F. F.-Y. and Wang, Q. (2006). Mothers' mastery-oriented involvement in children's homework: Implications for the well-being of children with negative perceptions of competence, *Journal of Educational Psychology* 98(1), 99.

Punter, R. A., Glas, C. A. and. Meelissen, M. R. (2016). Relation between parental involvement and student achievement in PIRLS-2011, *Psychometric Framework for Modeling Parental Involvement and Reading Literacy*, Springer, 77–87.

Roy, M. and Giraldo-García, R. (2018). The role of parental involvement and social/emotional skills in academic achievement: Global perspectives, *School Community Journal* 28(2), 29–46.

Sylva, K., Melhuish, E. C., Sammons, P., Siraj-Blatchford, I. and Taggart, B. (2004). The Effective Provision of Pre-School Education (EPPE) Project: Technical Paper 12 – The Final Report: Effective Pre-School Education. London, DfES/Institute of Education, University of London.

Sylva, K., Siraj-Blatchford, I. and Taggart, B. (2008). Final report from the primary phase: pre-school, school and family influences on children's development during key stage 2 (age 7–11), Sure Start.

Tett, L. (2001). Parents as problems or parents as people? Parental involvement programmes, schools and adult educators, *International Journal of Lifelong Education* 20(3), 188–198.

Thompson, I., Willemse, M., Mutton, T., Burn, K. and De Bruïne, E. (2018). Teacher education and family–school partnerships in different contexts: A cross country analysis of national teacher education frameworks across a range of European countries, *Journal of Education for Teaching*, 1–20.

Valencia, R. R. (2010). *Dismantling contemporary deficit thinking: Educational thought and practice*. New York, NY: Routledge.

Valencia, R. R. (2012). *The evolution of deficit thinking: Educational thought and practice*. New York, NY: Routledge.

Willemse, T. M., Thompson, I., Vanderlinde, R. and Mutton, T. (2018). 'Family-school partnerships: A challenge for teacher education, *Journal of Education for Teaching* 44(3), 252–257.

Wood, L. and Bauman, E. (2017). How family, school, and community engagement can improve student achievement and influence school reform. Washington, D.C.: American Institute for Research.

USING RESEARCH TO ENHANCE PARTNERSHIPS WITH PARENTS

DR GINA SHERWOOD

Gina Sherwood is an Associate Head at the University of Portsmouth and she applies her 20 years of teaching and training in Early Years as a Principal Lecturer. Her doctoral research focused on her practice in Early Years, exploring parents' experiences of support when they have a young child with a learning disability.

RESEARCH INTO PARTNERSHIP

This chapter focuses on an example of how to carry out research on partnership relationships with parents and carers in your setting. A starting point in all research is to identify a problem, and an honest review of partnership relationships between the main carer and the professional can highlight challenges and complexity. The content that follows explains how the research I did uncovered uncomfortable truths that led to recommendations to improve practice in Early Years settings.

WHY PARTNERSHIP IN EARLY YEARS?

A commitment to work in partnership with parents is not a new concept to anyone working in Early Years. Indeed, the central position of parents has been clarified both outside and within practice and is embedded in the Statutory Framework for the Early

Years Foundation Stage (EYFS) (DCSF, 2008; DfE, 2017). The EYFS seeks to provide 'partnership working between practitioners and with parents and/or carers' (p. 5), and this places the overarching principles of positive relationships and enabling environments at the forefront. In 2019 cultural capital was introduced and is now included within the Ofsted Inspection framework (Ofsted, 2019). In practice the aim of this measure is to apply an understanding of the child's culture and use it as a starting point for planning their next steps to ensure that the child reaches their potential. Parents have important information to facilitate this, and so research to identify ways to enhance relationships between them and your setting is essential to outstanding practice.

The rationale for building partnership is also reflected in research and government policy explaining that parental involvement in Early Years settings and schools improves academic outcomes for all children (Allen, 2011; DFE, 2015; Desforges and Abouchaar, 2003). The reason that a relationship of listening and working with parents is essential is that parents are understood to have significantly greater knowledge of their child than do professionals (Paige-Smith, 2010).

HOW TO RESEARCH PARTNERSHIP RELATIONSHIPS

The research that I undertook was with parents who had a young child with a learning disability. This experience led to methods and findings that can be used to address issues and solutions that are relevant to partnership relationships in any Early Years setting. I chose personal conversation to gather information so that I could hear about the lives of the parents I spoke to and learn a new way to think about and understand their position and predicament. When carrying out this type of investigation, the parent/main carer is central, and so it is essential to consider how they will be supported during the research and how to portray their voice faithfully. Applying these principles leads to findings that are authentic, with the potential to shape practice in future.

Many researchers set out with the intention of doing research 'on' their 'subjects', but I chose to take an alternative position and carry out my investigation 'with' the parents. To identify with their experiences and include my own reflections, I decided to include my thoughts and reactions alongside theirs. This enabled me to recognise my responses and assumptions and I could then see how these thoughts might become a barrier to understanding and empathising with their situation. My intention was to report not only their stories of what happened, but stories of what happened; what it felt like then; what it feels like in the telling; and how it takes on new meaning on the page as something to be reflected upon in a new, shared process (Sherwood and Nind, 2015).

In practice this type of research meant getting alongside each parent and being conscious of the influences and emotions affecting how they shared details of their lives and the impact of my role as a 'presence, ... listening and questioning in particular ways' (Riessman, 2008, p. 50). The plan at the heart of this research was to listen to the parent and to my inner voice and record both. I realised that I needed to be clear and honest about the reason for our conversations, so I shared the following points:

1. My intention was to learn something about how they experienced partnership and I didn't know exactly what the result would be.
2. The time that I would spend with them would give me a chance to understand their situation better and to reflect on how my feelings and interpretations could get in the way of building positive connections.
3. I intended to publish and talk about what they told me to enhance practice in the future.

When you are embarking of this type of research, it is important to be clear to the parent/main carer as to the reasons for your questions and to explain how information will be stored and used. Remember to let them know what you intend to report and explain that they can change their mind and withdraw from the project. Asking a parent to choose an alternative name helps to protect their anonymity. Being clear about your role and theirs enables them to see that you intend to listen to their story whilst compiling your own. It is essential to choose a place where they are comfortable to talk; select a location where you cannot be overheard and both you and the parent/main carer feel safe.

So that you can give the parent your full attention, I suggest that you ask their permission to audio record the conversation. This has the advantage of enabling you to listen back to what they have shared with you. I recommend that when you write up the key points you have heard from the conversation, you show them to the parents to check that they are accurate and that they are happy for the content to be distributed more widely. It is important to remind them that once the details have been published the reaction of those hearing and reading them is beyond your control (Riessman, 2008).

Alongside collecting information from listening to parents and to capture 'your story', I suggest that you keep a journal with notes about what is going through your mind and your feelings about what the parents tell you. This is called *co-construction*, because it is a process of recording a blend of descriptions and analysis, focusing on individuals (you and them) to understand their experience of events alongside your reactions (see Hitchcock and Hughes, 1995). You will find that the story that emerges is unique, shaped by the parent's experiences, personal definitions, assumptions and expectations. Suggesting that you meet with them again at a later stage enables you to implement changes in your setting and to assess their impact going forward.

The process of analysis takes time and means revisiting the conversations several times so that you can identify the most important parts of the parent's story and your own. I suggest that you share the information and interpretations with colleagues so that you can devise a plan together. Remember that honesty and transparency are key to achieving an authentic and useful picture of the life of the parent and their experience of interacting with your Early Years setting.

WHAT I FOUND OUT AND HOW IT CAN SHAPE PRACTICE

Table 1: Profile of 3 of the participants in my study

Parent	Child	Learning disability
Alfred: Father (32) Andrea: Mother (26) Unemployed, living in Local Authority housing.	Amber 3	Autism and chromosome disorder
Ruby: Mother (33) Unemployed, living in privately owned ex-Local Authority housing.	Reece 3	Speech and language delay

In this section I will provide extracts from my findings which are a blend of what the parent told me and reflections that are taken from my journal. I conclude each section with recommendations of how the information can be used to enhance partnership relationships. (To help readers understand the context of each family, these are set out in Table 1.)

The first interviews took place with **Alfred and Andrea** together, and the analysis reflects the impact of relationships when support services are involved. They provide an explanation of how some partnerships between the professional and parent are experienced.

Alfred gives the impression that he relies on Andrea. He writes 'wife no. 1' on his picture of the dartboard recording examples of support. The information he gives me infers that each has a specific role, for example, when talking about portage he says 'my wife does the most of it'. He appears to categorise certain people as being expert in particular areas, telling me that the family support worker (FSW) gives him advice on things he can't talk to his wife about. He explains that (in his opinion) the FSW is impartial, as he says: 'I've got someone not representing anyone else.' As he shared these stories of searching for someone to rescue him from his difficulties and perhaps 'tell him what to do', I found myself considering the role of the expert model in partnership. This partnership exists with the agreement of both parties, one seeking help, the other regarding themselves as qualified to tell the person what to do. In Alfred's case, his wife and the FSW have agreed to provide solutions for Alfred, and in doing so the identity of the expert is reinforced.

Meeting Andrea tested my pre-held opinions of what parents are looking for from support and illustrated the importance of listening to find out what living her life might be like. Through listening – to what was and was not said, searching below the surface – assumptions of how a parent in Andrea's positon might feel were challenged.

As we began the first interview, Andrea seemed conscious and proud of her role as someone who had all the information about Amber at her fingertips. Her body language, sitting up straight, steady eye contact, suggested she wanted to impress me. She told me in a clear, unemotional voice that Amber 'had huge behavioural problems'. This was her reason for rating KIDS number one in her 'top ten hits'. Her examples of what they do (offering advice on behaviour management strategies) seemed poignant, as I felt she wanted me to know that living with Amber was difficult, at the same time suggesting she was up to the challenge. I was left feeling – 'I'm not sure I would be'. Her priorities are the importance of Amber learning life skills first and education second. I wondered if this represented a resignation that her daughter would not achieve a great deal academically but that the life skills would bring about independence. However, her matter of fact tone taught me not to get carried away in my own interpretation of this being a tragedy.

When I revisited Alfred and Andrea over the three months, I began to experience feelings of unease – even frustration – in the apparent contradictions in their experiences of meeting professionals.

I noted the colourful language that was applied to both positive and negative encounters. In my first meeting Alfred tells me the staff at KIDS are: 'friendly, brilliant, well mannered', yet in the third interview I hear that: 'There's no one around who wants to help the parents. They will try and help the children but then it's very difficult because we haven't been getting the help that we should have been getting for our children.' A similar swing is communicated by Andrea, who tells me that after she challenged the response of the first health visitor who told her there was nothing wrong with Amber, 'we've got all the help we've needed really'. Yet at the third meeting I am confronted with another reality as Andrea tells me of her disappointment in professionals: 'They do not know your up from your down and your left from your right or anything like that' – her desperation as she tells me that they 'never answer what you need them to answer'.

I recorded the impact of these interactions, writing:

So often I note that what seems to represent a randomness sits uncomfortably with me. There is a lack of predictability and control which I know I rely on. It is only by attempting to enter her world, to form a bond of trust with Andrea, that the previous determined and authoritative mask she wears begins to slip, revealing a mixture of resentment, confusion, disappointment and helplessness as she tells me that professionals do not recognise 'her social phobia', thinking she is 'talking out of her bottom'. These truths are held carefully under wraps, leaving me feeling privileged that Andrea is able to share something of her vulnerability with me. Yet the fact that this provoked feelings of disturbance in me leaves me wondering how the truth would be received by another professional in my position.

These snapshots of Andrea's and Alfred's world tell us something about how complex parents' lives can be. When it comes to putting partnership relationships into practice, they clearly want someone they can trust and who will provide consistent support. Andrea wanted to feel understood, to be heard and to have her questions answered honestly. In reviewing my reactions I found that by being honest in my response I could see what needed to change in my approach and the judgements I had previously been making.

Ruby's story revealed more about partnership relationships. She wanted staff to give her more information about what Reece had been doing in pre-school, because he couldn't tell her himself because of his speech and language delay . She feared being labelled by professionals and negative implications for Reece.

> Ruby thinks if she phoned up the pre-school they would say, 'Oh, here we go.' Looking down and changing her pace of speech, she slowly tells me: 'I was worried they would treat him differently because he had that delay.' I ask her to explain what she means and she stumbles over an answer, saying: 'I didn't want them to sort of pick on him and ... I know that sounds terrible, but um you know I didn't want them to sort of, you know? Not focus on him as much, you know?' This concern she said arose from reading 'horror stories about nurseries', wondering if they might 'isolate him as such'. As I realised Ruby's fears for her son, I felt shock and imagined that these thoughts were hidden from the professionals, covered by her apparently jovial and informal communication style.

As Krauss (2000) explains, the success of working in partnership that leads to effective intervention for children and their families depends on a relationship that is shaped by the attitudes and definitions of those around them. Rix and Paige-Smith (2011) recommend honesty, so that contradictions and struggles become a starting point for reflecting on practice and personal perspectives.

CONCLUSION

The process of listening to the parents' stories and writing my own became a teacher in unexpected ways (Sherwood and Nind, 2014). I was able to uncover information about the fears, needs and priorities of parents. It taught me to avoid making assumptions and to build in more regular checkpoints to hear how the parent is doing. I realised that I needed to review the idea that the parent was a potential problem and reframe the relationship to work with them in partnership to find solutions for them and their child.

TOP TIPS

- Partnership with the child's main carer is essential, and carrying out research with them reveals the complexity of their lives and experiences.
- When you immerse yourself in their story and identify your own reactions, you can reflect on the origins of your thoughts and feelings and address barriers to building a successful partnership.
- Listening to the parent and your inner voice can lead to an honest review of processes and practices in your setting, what works well and what needs to change.

REFERENCE LIST

Allen, G. (2011). Early Intervention: The Next Steps. London: The Cabinet Office.

DCSF (2008). The Early Years Foundation Stage: Setting the standards for learning, development and care for children from birth to five. In Department for Children, Schools and Families (eds), DCSF.

Desforges, C. and Abouchaar, A. (2003). The impact of parental involvement, parental support and family education on pupil achievement and adjustment, a literature review. London, DfES.

DfE (2015). Disability and Special Educational Needs Code of Practice: 0–25 years. Retrieved from https://assets.publishing.service.gov.uk/government/uploads/system/uploads/attachment_data/file/398815/SEND_Code_of_Practice_January_2015.pdf.

DfE (2017). Statutory Framework for the Early Years Foundation Stage: Setting the standards for learning, development and care for children birth to five. Retrieved from https://assets.publishing.service.gov.uk/government/uploads/system/uploads/attachment_data/file/596629/EYFS_STATUTORY_FRAMEWORK_2017.pdf.

Hitchcock, G. and Hughes, D. (1995). *Research and the teacher*, 2nd edition. London: Routledge.

Krauss, M. W. (2000). Family assessment within early intervention programs. In J. P. Shonkoff and S. J. Meisels, *Handbook of early childhood intervention*, 2nd edition, 290–308. Cambridge: Cambridge University Press.

Ofsted (2019). Early Years Inspection Handbook for Ofsted Registered Provision. Retrieved from https://assets.publishing.service.gov.uk/government/uploads/system/uploads/attachment_data/file/828465/Early_years_inspection_handbook.pdf.

Paige-Smith, A. (2010). Parent partnership and inclusion in early years. In L. Miller, C. Cable and G. Goodliff (eds), *Supporting children's learning in the Early Years*, 2nd edition, 39–47. London: David Fulton.

Riessman, C. K. (2008). *Narrative methods for the human sciences*. London: Sage.

Rix, J. and Paige-Smith, A. (2011). Exploring barriers to reflection and learning – Developing a perspective lens, *Journal of Research in Special Educational Needs* 11, 30–41.

Sherwood, G. and Nind, M. A. (2014). Parents' experience of support: Co-constructing their stories, *International Journal of Early Years Education* 22(4), 457–470. doi.org/10.1080/09669760.2014.970520.

GOOD LEADERSHIP IN EARLY YEARS: A BLUE-PRINT FOR GETTING YOUR HOME IN ORDER

LEWIS FOGARTY

Lewis Fogarty is a Director of Always Growing, a small group of Early Years provisions in Berkshire. Alongside this, he lectures in Leadership and Management on the MA Education programme at Brunel University. This is also where he is completing his EdD, developing a new construction of leadership in Early Years through participatory research into the lived experiences of Early Years practitioners.

INTRODUCTION

In this chapter I will draw on a familiar analogy of your setting being like a home, built on solid foundations, supported by a secure structure and a protective roof, to set out my research-informed framework that can inspire shared purpose and good leadership in Early Years settings. I call this the Four Pillars of Pedagogy (4POP) framework and draw on a range of research that contributed to its construction and implementation in my setting. With a clear framework like the 4POP, coupled with the passion that is ubiquitous in the Early Years workforce, I hope this chapter supports more settings to 'get their home in order' and embark on a reflective, research-informed journey towards good leadership. Through good leadership, meaningful and continuous development can occur and the sector as a whole can be elevated.

A CONFUSED AND TENSION-LADEN SECTOR

From my experience, there is a need to seek order in the confusing environment within which Early Years is situated, and turning to research is a way of making sense of this messiness. There has been on average one major policy change per year for the last 30 years, altering the way we work in the sector dramatically (Nutbrown and Clough, 2013). These changes have altered funding and regulatory measures and have created an uneven playing field for the dynamic and wide-ranging providers that make up the childcare market in the UK.

The resultant reality for these providers is one that has an overriding tension between education and care, with far-reaching consequences for purpose and pedagogy in the ongoing play vs school readiness debate in the sector. I make sense of this through Bernstein's (2000) official recontextualising field (ORF) and pedagogic recontextualising field (PRF) dichotomy, which identifes the transformation of discourse into practice as the pivotal moment of pedagogy. The ORF mechanisms are directed by the state and its representatives through policy and white papers, whereas the PRF mechanisms are directed by specialist practitioners in the workforce. Those in the PRF wholeheartedly advocate for play, as pioneers such as Susan Isaacs highlighted that play is a child's life and the means by which children explore and come to understand the world around them (Mickelburgh, 2018). Thus, play should not be compromised by the school readiness movement. Bernstein (2000) suggests that the ORF is attempting to weaken the PRF and therefore professional autonomy in education; I am sure many practitioners would agree they experience this ongoing tension on a daily basis, particularly with the additional economic pressures applied on the sector during the pandemic.

As a profession, practitioners need to resist the overt forces of the ORF, which makes books like this all the more important. I am of the belief that this resistance requires collective effort and all individuals to be leaders (Bolden et al., 2008). This move away from traditional hierarchical understandings of leadership is supported elsewhere by Nicholson et al. (2018), who state that the traditional notion of leadership being reserved for those at the top with formal authority is at odds with the purpose and context of Early Years. Through empowering more individuals to enact leadership responsibility, there could be a greater sense of professional confidence, described by Bradbury et al. (forthcoming) as when individuals are not simply victims of policy but are able to maintain professional pride and quality in their provision. With more professional confidence in the sector, questioning and resisting the impact of policy can be stronger and focus can remain on what matters most in a sector that is increasingly underappreciated (Lloyd, 2018; Bonetti, 2020).

Despite being in this complex and confused sector, together battling the influence of the ORF, Early Years settings often face a unique set of challenges specific to their own individual context. Therefore, it is essential to remember that they are the expert in their own home, with the children in their care. I don't mean 'their home' to imply the sector is only made up of home-based providers, which are an integral part of the sector. I mean it to imply that each setting can be seen as a home, which I will explain in more detail now.

All good homes are built on solid foundations, and for me this refers to a broad yet clearly defined sense of educational purpose. Biesta (2015) sets out three domains of educational purpose: qualification, referring to the transmission and acquisition of knowledge and skills; socialisation, referring to the importance of initiating learners into cultural, religious and professional traditions; and subjectification, referring to the importance of learners becoming empowered and responsible individuals. Whilst the ORF and the perpetuating government initiatives drive unabatedly towards the domain of qualification, the professionals within the education sector must resist and make professional judgements to ensure balance in the approach they adopt in their setting.

Every home also has a specific roof built to size, and this refers to the policies and procedures that every setting develops and tweaks specifically to their context, drawing on up-to-date research literature and updates from local and central government. When working with valuable people such as Early Years children, there is no excuse for not having robust and up-to-date policies that all practitioners are trained in and familiar with in order to keep themselves and all other stakeholders safe.

The final part of the home analogy is the pillars surrounding it, which is where my 4POP framework demarcates the secure space within which the magic of Early Years can happen.

THE 4POP FRAMEWORK AS A BLUEPRINT FOR YOUR SETTING
The 4POP is rooted in my experiences of leading my own Early Years organisation, and I hope it can be something readers can draw on to apply in their own contexts:

1. reassuring relationships – the heartbeat of my philosophy that needs to be present between teachers and learners to promote a sense of care that makes everyone feel safe and able to engage in learning
2. clear communication – a fundamental feature of any relationship that is often not given enough consideration; this includes actively listening to, as well as giving, information
3. continuous curiosity – this links to the notion of being a life-long learner, something practitioners in the Early Years should be role modelling, sharing challenges and success along the way
4. enabling environment – an environment that is welcoming and stimulating is essential for individuals to develop their own thinking and to encourage the other three pillars of pedagogy.

In my organisation all team members are introduced to this during their induction through our culture manual. It's also a central part of most development-focused communication and the appraisal cycle, with everyone receiving a target related to each of the pillars (including me!). It forms the basis for a shared language that everyone understands and can relate their everyday practice to. For example, we can discuss the impact of 4POP just in the first five minutes of children entering our setting. Each child will receive a unique welcome that is reassuring and familiar and they will be reminded clearly through signs and by the team to wash their hands. Upon returning from the toilet, they will be able to explore a range of provocations to spark their curiosity, within a secure environment that is familiar enough to make the individuals feel safe, yet transient enough to engage them each day in a range of activities.

A central thesis for this chapter is that through linking this framework with research and innovative understandings of leadership, all individuals can be empowered to, and accountable for, enacting their own individual leadership responsibility. I will now turn my attention towards addressing this linkage more directly.

A CALL FOR GOOD LEADERSHIP

I have already hinted at the importance of moving away from hierarchical understandings of leadership. But if not a hierarchical understanding, then what? Drath et al. (2008) suggest a move towards a focus on outcomes of direction, alignment and commitment, which they state are more likely to be realised in the presence of effective leadership behaviours. This then leads to the question, what are effective leadership behaviours? From my experience, I would suggest that a leader who distributes leadership responsibility amongst their team – through appropriate accountability and empowerment measures – would be on the right path. For this to be effective, leaders need to develop a shared language among their team which could be centred around the 4POP framework.

Setting a clear direction is a primary role of a leader, in a hierarchical sense or not. This direction, of course, needs to be contextual. Penn (2019) suggests that leadership is always contextual and that context is driven by purpose. This purpose should be a broad and balanced approach to education and care, drawing on the work previously explored by Biesta (2015) and the latest statutory guidance in the EYFS. Encouraging alignment can be achieved through a clear induction and appraisal process, which can be framed by the 4POP. A shared understanding of leadership also encourages support and challenge in equal measure, and this inclusive nature of operating will naturally encourage alignment. Commitment to their work is, I think, a quality that is inherent in almost all Early Years practitioners. Those who do not have this sense of commitment quickly realise how important it is to the role and that they were either misinformed or wholeheartedly erroneous if they assumed their job would be an easy one. However, tackling this issue is outside the scope of this chapter.

Within the scope of this chapter is the development of the theme of striving for good leadership in Early Years. Sims and Waniganayake (2015, p. 190) stated that 'those who are the most effective leaders are those who self-identify as leaders'. This idea is predicated on the idea that leaders have a strong internalised identity and clear behavioural intentions. Considering the ubiquitous low status and pay construction of the workforce in tandem with the confusions and complexities of the sector, it is not surprising that to have a strong internalised identity and clear behavioural intentions is challenging. However, as previously mentioned, this can be supported through the nourishment of professional confidence.

Although I have written in some detail about leadership behaviour, I have not said enough about individuals' identity and the uniqueness of individuals in Early Years – a uniqueness arising not just from the challenges they face, but from who they are. The sector is around 96 per cent female and Ebbeck and Waniganayake (2003) suggest that many practitioners do not want to engage with leadership discussions involving power and authority, as they see it as irrelevant to working with children and their families. Unfortunately, this is a barrier that needs to be overcome to develop good leadership in the sector. Professional conversations that involve support, challenging problematising policy and resisting extraneous workload on teams need to become commonplace in Early Years settings. This is everyone's responsibility. Interestingly, Gilligan (1982) suggests that women speak in a different voice, and it can be said that women generally prize caring, nurturing and the formation of interpersonal community. Therefore, connection needs to be made between the caring and nurturing nature of much of the workforce and the characteristics needed to feel empowered as part of a collaborative leadership community.

This is complemented by Helgesen's approach to leadership coined as the Web of Inclusion (1990). This is an activist form of leadership striving for an environment where everyone can thrive. It is an environment that is connected and integrated, like a community. Within this organisational structure, there can be new ways of thinking about leadership responsibility, where knowledge construction is contextualised, socially constituted and dynamic (Nicholson et al., 2018) and therefore the leader needs to be in the centre, in the thick of things, connected to others for support, growth and sustainability – a notion that is particularly pertinent in Early Years in the current climate.

CONCLUSION

I solemnly hope this chapter has given you new ways to think and talk about leadership and development in your setting. Leadership should not be seen as a responsibility reserved for the person that sits at the top of the hierarchy, so if that person is you, then you have an important role in instilling leadership responsibility throughout your organisation through suitable accountability and empowerment structures. The work of Helgesen (1990) or Drath et al. (2008) may provide a framework for this necessary change.

I also hope you see the potential that a clear framework such as the 4POP could have in supporting how you talk about the best parts of your practice, as well as the areas that need to be developed. Most importantly, I hope that you do something as a result of reading this chapter. Whilst this could well be one of the top tips I indicate below, I hope you leave this page with a sense of strength, a heightened professional confidence and a willingness to advocate for change that could ultimately improve the lives of the children and colleagues in your extremely important and unique Early Years setting.

TOP TIPS

- Reflect on how you frame the outstanding work you do in your setting – does your team speak with a shared language? Maybe 4POP could help with that.
- Be curious and inspire curiosity in all of your stakeholders. You could join Twitter as a starting point and follow everyone who contributed to this book – you don't need to share anything at first if you don't want to; just be a sponge!
- Consistently support and challenge those around you in a positive and purposeful manner.

REFERENCES

Bernstein, B. (2000). *Pedagogy, symbolic control and identity*, revised edition. Washington DC: Rowman & Littlefield Publishers.

Biesta, G. (2015). What is education for? On good education, teacher judgement, and educational professionalism, *European Journal of Education* 50(1), 75–87. DOI:10.1111/ejed.12109.

Bolden, R., Petrov, G. and Gosling, J. (2008). *Developing Collective Leadership in Higher Education. Centre for Leadership Studies.* Retrieved from https://www.advance-he.ac.uk/knowledge-hub/developing-collective-leadership-higher-education.

Bonetti, S. (2020, August 5). Early years are overworked and underappreciated, *TES*. Retrieved from https://www.tes.com/news/early-years-are-overworked-and-underappreciated.

Bradbury, A., Hoskins, K. and Fogarty, L. (Forthcoming). Policy actors in a hostile environment: The views of staff in nursery schools in England, *Journal of Education Policy*.

Drath, W. H., Cynthia, D., McCauley, C. J. P., Van Velsor, E., O'Connor, P. M. G. and McGuire, J. B. (2008). Direction, alignment, commitment: Toward a more integrative ontology of leadership, *The Leadership Quarterly* 19, 635–653.

Ebbeck, M. and Waniganayake, M. (2003). *Early childhood professionals: Leading today and tomorrow.* Sydney, NSW: MacLennan & Petty.

Gilligan, C. (1982). *In a different voice: Psychological theory and women's development.* Cambridge, Mass and London: Harvard University Press.

Helgesen, S. (1990). *The female advantage: Women's ways of leadership.* New York, NY: Doubleday Currency.

Helgesen, S. (2005). *The web of inclusion: Architecture for building great organizations.* New York, NY: Doubleday.

Lloyd, E. (20 April 2018). Underpaid and undervalued: The reality of childcare work in the UK, *The Conversation.* Retrieved from https://theconversation.com/underpaid-and-undervalued-the-reality-of-childcare-work-in-the-uk-87413.

Mickelburgh, J. (18 March 2018). Educational Pioneers: Susan Isaacs, 1885–1948. Foundation stage forum. Retrieved from https://eyfs.info/articles.html/teaching-and-learning/educational-pioneers-susan-isaacs-1885-1948-r40/.

Nicholson, J., Kuhl, K., Maniates, H., Lin, B. and Bonetti, S. (2018). A review of the literature on leadership in early childhood: Examining epistemological foundations and considerations of social justice, *Early Child Development and Care* 1–32. DOI: 10.1080/03004430.2018.1455036.

Nutbrown, C. and Clough, P. (2013). *Inclusion in the Early Years: Critical analysis and enabling narratives.* Thousand Oaks, CA: Sage.

Penn, H. (2019). Understanding the contexts of leadership debates, *Contemporary Issues in Early Childhood* 20(1), 104–109.

Sims, M. & Waniganayake, M. (2015). The role of staff in quality improvement in early childhood, *Journal of Education and Training Studies* 3(5), 187–194.

DEVELOPING EARLY YEARS PEDAGOGY THROUGH CRITICALLY REFLECTIVE PRACTICE: A RETROSPECTIVE

SUE ROGERS

Sue Rogers is a Professor of Early Years Education. She has held several senior roles, including most recently Interim Director of the UCL Institute of Education. Before moving into higher education, Sue worked as an Early Years and primary school teacher. Since gaining her PhD in 2000, Sue has researched and published widely on the relationship between play and pedagogy in Early Years classrooms, outdoor play and learning and, more recently, effective professional learning approaches in the Early Years workforce.

INTRODUCTION: IN THE BEGINNING

I began my professional life as a teacher of young children some 30 years ago, initially working in a Reception class in a rural primary school. From the very beginning, I was fascinated by the ways in which children learn and develop in early childhood and how schools and Early Years settings either support or constrain that learning. Each afternoon, 'my' children would play freely, selecting from and combining a range of resources, which I provided in zoned areas much like you see today in Early Years settings. From time to time, I would roll out a carpet and invite children to join me on a journey. We would 'fly' to imagined places, adopt roles and create collective stories.

These magic carpet journeys were amongst the most memorable moments of my teaching career, and our imaginary adventures would often turn up days later in the children's role play or in their written stories.

Growing out of that play-based approach to teaching, I became increasingly interested to know more about how Early Years pedagogy can support children's learning in play. At that time, Early Years or pre-school and Reception were of relatively little interest to policymakers and curriculum theorists. Planning for children under five was more a matter of applying principles to practice. Research on young children in the context of school was underdeveloped and perceived by some as low status at that time, a perception that has been difficult to shift until relatively recently. But over time, there was growing recognition that the education of young children needed a stronger research base to support it and that there was little in the way of firm evidence to take from the early childhood tradition. Early Years practice was described as a 'common law', highlighting the extent to which work in Early Years at that time was based more on an inherited tradition than on classroom-based 'evidence' of the most effective ways to teach young children.

Against this background, in this chapter I offer a few reflections on how my work and the Early Years field has changed, and why this book is timely in the way that it draws together chapters from a range of professionals with a common purpose: to deploy the best possible research evidence in ways that have practical value and make a positive difference to the education of young children.

Looking back, my very first research project was shaped to a large extent by the call to understand better why we taught in particular ways and how children learned as a consequence – in its time it might also be thought of as a revolution! The topic of my part-time PhD (1996–2000) was a study of the perspectives on play held by Early Years teachers and how these were enacted in practice. Few if any studies of play or Early Years practice sought to involve practitioners in reflective dialogue or in sharing their perspectives on practice.

First, the predominant meanings ascribed to play and applied in classrooms stemmed principally from psycho-biological research as seen, for example, in the widespread and often oversimplified application of the work of Piagetian stages to young children's education (see also Chapter 6). Second, alongside this body of knowledge, Early Years education drew heavily on its history and inheritance – its roots in a mostly eighteenth and nineteenth century philosophy of child-centred education exemplified in the works of Rousseau and other 'pioneer' educators such as Maria Montessori and Susan Isaacs.

My doctoral work enabled me to investigate the ways in which these two intellectual currents shaped the thinking and practice of play in Early Years classrooms. They gave only a partial account of how the contexts of education shape the experience of play for children and the nature of teachers' pedagogy. Teaching and learning are, of course, much more complex than that, and, as I attempted to demonstrate, might be thought of as the locus of interactions between the needs of the teacher and the needs of the child, between ideological and pragmatic imperatives, between the spontaneous and intrinsically motivated actions of the child and the demands of the externally regulated curricular framework. From here, I began to formulate my thinking on the conceptual and empirical distinctions between play on the one hand and pedagogy on the other (Rogers, 2011), and where, if any, were the points of contact.

EARLY YEARS PEDAGOGY: A QUIET REVOLUTION

As we can see from the reflections shared in several of the chapters of this book, much has changed in the intervening decades since my own early work in the fields of play research and Early Years pedagogy. The Early Years profession has in many respects 'come of age', with a richer, more diverse research and evidence base on Early Years practice and a much greater emphasis on professional learning and development of the workforce.

At the same time, like Dominic Wyse in Chapter 8 of this book, I would want to caution against viewing research evidence and its use in a narrow, uncontextualised way or as the panacea for the many challenges faced in working with young children and their families. As Wyse argues, one of the most important elements about being research-informed is 'to realise that it requires the *interpretation* of research followed by *choices* and decisions about how to respond.'

The recent emphasis placed on professional learning in Early Years, and particularly that which promotes critical reflection and focuses on the use and interpretation of research in the classroom, is very welcome in this respect. The concept of 'reflective practice', though by no means new to the teaching profession, is also firmly embedded in the statutory guidance for the Early Years Foundation Stage (EYFS) and is a requirement in all levels of training for Early Years professionals.

Critical reflection on research evidence can allow Early Years professionals to deepen awareness and understanding of how young children learn, grow and develop in an ongoing process of improving quality of provision. It may lead to a pedagogic role that is more finely tuned to children's needs and interests (Rose and Rogers, 2012). How we view children as learners is also informed by our own values, beliefs and experiences. These shape our pedagogical practices and the ways in which we interact with children, and hence impact upon children's experience of the Early Years setting.

As I found in my own research, part of the challenge in providing a play-based pedagogy is coping with the uncertainty and ambiguity of play in the learning environment. Providing for play may be challenging for some practitioners because of its difficult-to-measure and potentially difficult-to-manage qualities (Rogers, 2014). But research projects have shown that reflecting on this uncertainty in trusting, reciprocal relationships with other professionals can enhance insight into and confidence in practice and can be empowering to bring professionals' knowledge of and principles about children into closer alignment with the challenging aspects of their work. In addition, the external context is ever present in the classroom: pedagogy is shaped by particular political and cultural contexts, which ultimately can either inhibit or support children's potential and progression in learning and development. A research-informed profession can build advocacy for young children and their families.

BECOMING RESEARCH-INFORMED THROUGH PROFESSIONAL LEARNING

Fast forward some two decades since completion of my PhD to a number of projects that illustrate the ways in which shared reflection and problem-solving can improve outcomes for young children. In each case, projects were informed by the question: How can we make research evidence matter in the context of Early Years pedagogical practice? The central aim of these projects, to improve outcomes for children, particularly those most at risk of disadvantage, deployed best available research evidence on effective pedagogy to support the EYFS characteristics of effective learning (DfE, 2020). Through making research accessible and relatable to practice, the projects aimed to empower Early Years practitioners through a combination of engagement with research evidence *and* opportunities to identify and address pedagogical issues in practice, in a critically reflective and collaborative way. One of the strengths and positive aspects of these projects was the way in which they brought together Early Years professionals from a range of different settings and age groups. So, for example, Reception class teachers worked with children's centre educators. One children's centre educator explained that:

We all come from different places ... with different qualifications ... some have degrees, some haven't ...but what I have learned is that we're all here for the same outcome, to educate the children with the best practice.

In this way the experience of *shared* reflection on practice served to build a much stronger sense of community amongst Early Years professionals in the group over many months, breaking down barriers between pre-school and school and between differently qualified staff. Working in this way also enabled professionals from both University research and Early Years practice backgrounds to share knowledge and expertise and find joint solutions to pedagogical challenges (Brown and Rogers, 2014). A significant factor in the success of these projects was duration and intensity of learning. Monthly workshops, provision of reading, and opportunities to try things out in the Early Years setting not only consolidated the learning community over time, but enabled deeper learning to take place. The participants were better able to reflect upon tensions arising from sustaining play-based provision and draw upon a body of evidence to support their principles for the education of young children, and to balance these with the statutory requirements placed upon them.

In a more recent project, a systematic review of research into effective professional learning in the Early Years sector (Rogers et al., 2020) asked the question: What approaches to professional development and learning are most effective for improving the knowledge and skills of the EYE [Early Years Education] workforce and so improve outcomes for young children? The project team reviewed over a thousand papers from across the globe.

First, there were almost no studies capable of measuring the impact of professional learning on children in the Early Years conducted in the UK. This in itself indicates the underdeveloped nature of the field. Thus, we were reliant on extracting findings from studies conducted mainly in the USA and cross referencing these with studies in the UK school system. From these studies, the message was clear and perhaps not surprising. The most effective approaches to professional learning are those that combine new knowledge and research findings with opportunities for reflection and scaffolded interaction through facilitated workshops and coaching. Also important is that research must be made accessible and relatable to the current practice and context of Early Years professionals, a point also noted by Bryce-Clegg in Chapter 6. Working with a 'coach' to identify how to address areas for development or to enhance how the approach may be further improved was highly effective, although peer-to-peer support can act in similar ways to help the development of practice. It would seem the most effective approaches reflect social constructivist models of effective learning.

Shared reflection in professional communities of practice offers a powerful vehicle for effecting change in play pedagogy (Rogers and Brown, 2014). Equally, however, we acknowledge the fact that opportunities for reflection in the Early Years sector are relatively rare because of limited time, funds and commitment on the part of school and setting leaders in spite of the fact that reflective practice is a statutory requirement in the EYFS. Early Years professionals have had little if any access to this type of high-quality Continuing Professional Development (CPD), and yet are de facto accountable to policymakers for so-called 'school readiness' and later achievement in school. The present book is testament to the 'long march' towards recognition of the importance of professional learning in the Early Years sector to move beyond the type of mandatory CPD concerned with regulatory and compliance issues such as health and safety, important though that is. As Julie Mountain notes in Chapter 10 of this book, the one-day 'pit-stop' professional learning is far less frequent now.

FINAL REFLECTIONS: BECOMING RESEARCH-INFORMED ADVOCATES FOR YOUNG CHILDREN

I want to end this chapter by returning to some fundamental questions about why we do what we do and in fact why there is a need for this book at all. Each of the chapters has in some way revisited the essence of what it means to be an Early Years educator but also demonstrated vividly, through examples, the potential of using research in practice to enhance and progress the experiences of young children. Some authors in this book, like me, can look back over several decades working in the Early Years sector and comment first hand on the very profound changes that have taken place. There are many areas of overlap between the chapters, not least the points made about the importance of collaboration, learning by looking beyond the school or setting and not becoming overly dependent on one or two research perspectives -- keep an open mind and avoid fads and fashions often offered as quick fixes on social media.

Firstly, I share so many of these viewpoints, but focusing in on my own personal 'clarion call' I would ask the reader to take a moment to reflect on the extent to which you make time to 'nourish' yourself and your practice. You might do this through reading and writing, observing practice or simply sharing the good, the bad and the ugly with colleagues. It is hugely demanding to work with young children, particularly in an educational context that very often conflicts with our values and principles, and not least currently as we grapple with a pandemic that has had a profound and lasting impact on the lives and the education of young children, both surfacing and exacerbating huge inequalities in our society. Make time for your own learning, and, as many other authors have noted, share your learning and insights with others through networks, both locally and in the many excellent social media groups. In other words, find your community of practice. It will be a great source of support at all points in your career.

Secondly, it perhaps goes without saying that it is a huge privilege to work with young children, to work with their unbounded curiosity and rapidly developing imaginative, social and physical capacities. But you will need to defend its importance and its complexity at times, and listen to comments from the less well informed that Early Years education is 'just playing' and is of lower status than teaching subjects in a secondary school. Of course, this is simply untrue. But being more research-informed is one of the best ways to challenge such assumptions with confidence. Being more knowledgeable can help us to become powerful advocates for young children and argue more persuasively for the importance of effective evidence-based professional learning opportunities.

Thirdly, and perhaps most important of all, when looking at evidence, keep the children in mind. What meaning does research have for your children and your practice in your setting? Here, I will refer back to the words of Bason-Wood in Chapter 9 of this book, which neatly captures my point and takes me back to the beginning of my career in teaching:

> Look at the awe and wonder in the children and absorb that for yourself. Keep the fun and never forget the reason you wanted to become an educator in the first place – to make a difference in young children's lives!

I would argue that even in the context of increasing regulation and 'schoolification' of Early Years practice, it is still possible to roll out the magic carpet!

REFERENCES

Brown, C. and Rogers, S. (2014). Knowledge Creation as an approach to facilitating evidence informed practice: Examining ways to measure the success of using this method with Early Years practitioners in Camden (London), *Journal of Educational Change*. DOI:10.1007/s10833-014-9238-9.

Rogers, S., Brown, C. and Poblete, X. (2020). A systematic review of professional learning in Early Years Education, *Review of Education*.

Rogers, S. (2014). Enabling pedagogy. In J. Moyles, J. Payler and J. Georgeson (eds), *Early Years Foundations: Meeting the challenge*. Maidenhead: Open University Press.

Rogers, S. and Brown, C. (2014). Transforming play pedagogy: Connecting Early Years practitioners with research evidence. In J. Moyles, (ed.), *The Excellence of Play*, 4th edition. Maidenhead: Open University Press.

Rogers, S. (2011). (ed.) *Rethinking play and pedagogy: Contexts, concepts and cultures*. London: Routledge.

Rogers, S. and Evans, J. (2008). *Inside role play in Early Childhood Education: Researching children's perspectives*. London: Routledge.

Rose, J. and Rogers, S. (2012). *Adult Roles in the Early Years*. Maidenhead: Open University Press.

REFERENCES